EDINBURGH

Travel with Marco Polo Insider Tips

INSIDER TIP Your shortcut to a great experience

MARCO POLO TOP HIGHLIGHTS

SCOTTISH PARLIAMENT ★
This impressive building, constructed at the turn of the century for a modern Scotland, provides a fascinating contrast to the Old Town.
📷 *Tip: An hour-long tour will provide you with unique perspectives for pictures.*

➤ p. 34, Sightseeing

EDINBURGH CASTLE ★
Perched on a hilltop, this landmark castle has been overlooking the city for the last 800 years.
📷 *Tip: A great place to get a photo of the castle is from the Miss Jean Brodie Steps at the Grassmarket.*

➤ p. 30, Sightseeing

SCOTTISH NATIONAL GALLERY OF MODERN ART ★
On the edge of an idyllic village, two neoclassical buildings contain art spanning the past 100 years.

➤ p. 47, Sightseeing

ROYAL MILE ★
Edinburgh's medieval mile runs from the castle to the Palace of Holyroodhouse, with many historic buildings along its route.
📷 *Tip: From the roof of the cathedral, you have a bird's eye view in both directions.*

➤ p. 28, Sightseeing

ARTHUR'S SEAT ★
The silhouette of this extinct volcano is one of the city's iconic sights. Climb its 250m peak for panoramic views of up to 100km on a clear day.

➤ p. 37, Sightseeing

GEORGE STREET ⭐

An upscale area ideal for shopping and strolling: the Fashion Mile, with proud Georgian architecture, is the New Town's answer to the Royal Mile.

➤ p. 72, Sightseeing

LEITH ⭐

The old port to the north of the Old Town is *the* place for going out: it has three Michelin-starred restaurants, street-food halls and a royal yacht.

➤ p. 47, Sightseeing &
p. 77, Nightlife

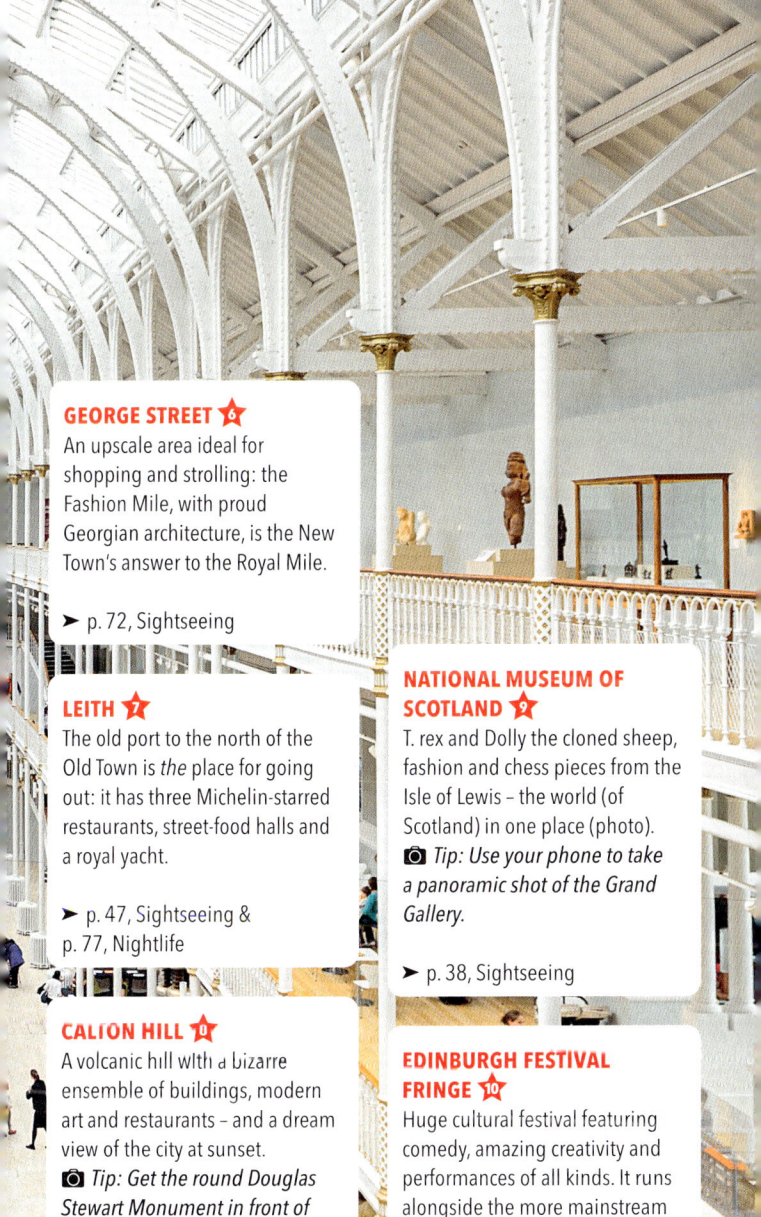

NATIONAL MUSEUM OF SCOTLAND ⭐

T. rex and Dolly the cloned sheep, fashion and chess pieces from the Isle of Lewis – the world (of Scotland) in one place (photo).
📷 *Tip: Use your phone to take a panoramic shot of the Grand Gallery.*

➤ p. 38, Sightseeing

CALTON HILL ⭐

A volcanic hill with a bizarre ensemble of buildings, modern art and restaurants – and a dream view of the city at sunset.
📷 *Tip: Get the round Douglas Stewart Monument in front of you and align your view of the castle for a great photo.*

➤ p. 44, Sightseeing

EDINBURGH FESTIVAL FRINGE ⭐

Huge cultural festival featuring comedy, amazing creativity and performances of all kinds. It runs alongside the more mainstream Edinburgh International Festival.

➤ p. 18, Sightseeing &
p. 93, Festivals & events

CONTENTS

⏲	Plan your visit	🍴	Eating/drinking	☂	Rainy day activities
£-£££	Price categories	🛍	Shopping	🐷	Budget activities
		🍸	Nightlife	🎭	Family activities
		🌴	Top beaches	🚩	Classic experiences

(📖 A2) Refers to the removable pull-out map

4

CONTENTS

MARCO POLO TOP HIGHLIGHTS
2   Top 10 highlights

BEST OF EDINBURGH
8   ... when it rains
9   ... on a budget
10   ... with children
11   ... classic experiences

GET TO KNOW EDINBURGH
14   Discover Edinburgh
17   At a glance
18   Understand Edinburgh
21   True or false?

24   SIGHTSEEING
28   Old Town
40   New Town
46   Other sights
50   Day trips

52   EATING & DRINKING

64   SHOPPING

76   NIGHTLIFE

ACTIVE & RELAXED
90   Sport & wellness
92   Festivals & events
94   Sleep well

DISCOVERY TOURS
100 Edinburgh at a glance
103 Idyll along the Water of Leith
106 Literary trail
111 Over the volcano

GOOD TO KNOW
114 **HOLIDAY BASICS**
     Arrival, Getting around, Emergencies, Essentials, Weather
122 **HOLIDAY VIBES**
     Books, films, music & blogs
124 **TRAVEL PURSUIT**
     The Marco Polo holiday quiz
126 **INDEX & CREDITS**
128 **DOS & DON'TS!**
     How to avoid slip-ups & blunders

BEST OF EDINBURGH

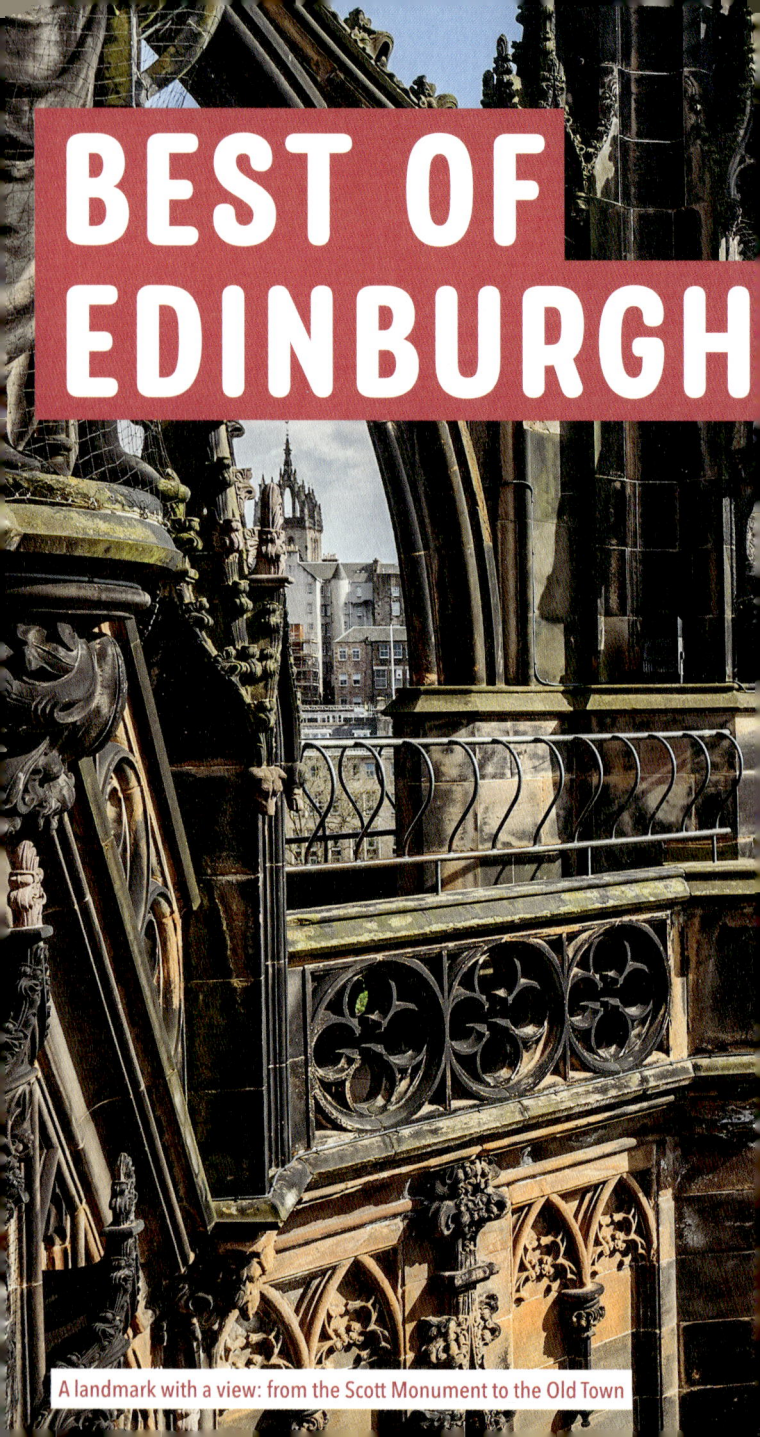

A landmark with a view: from the Scott Monument to the Old Town

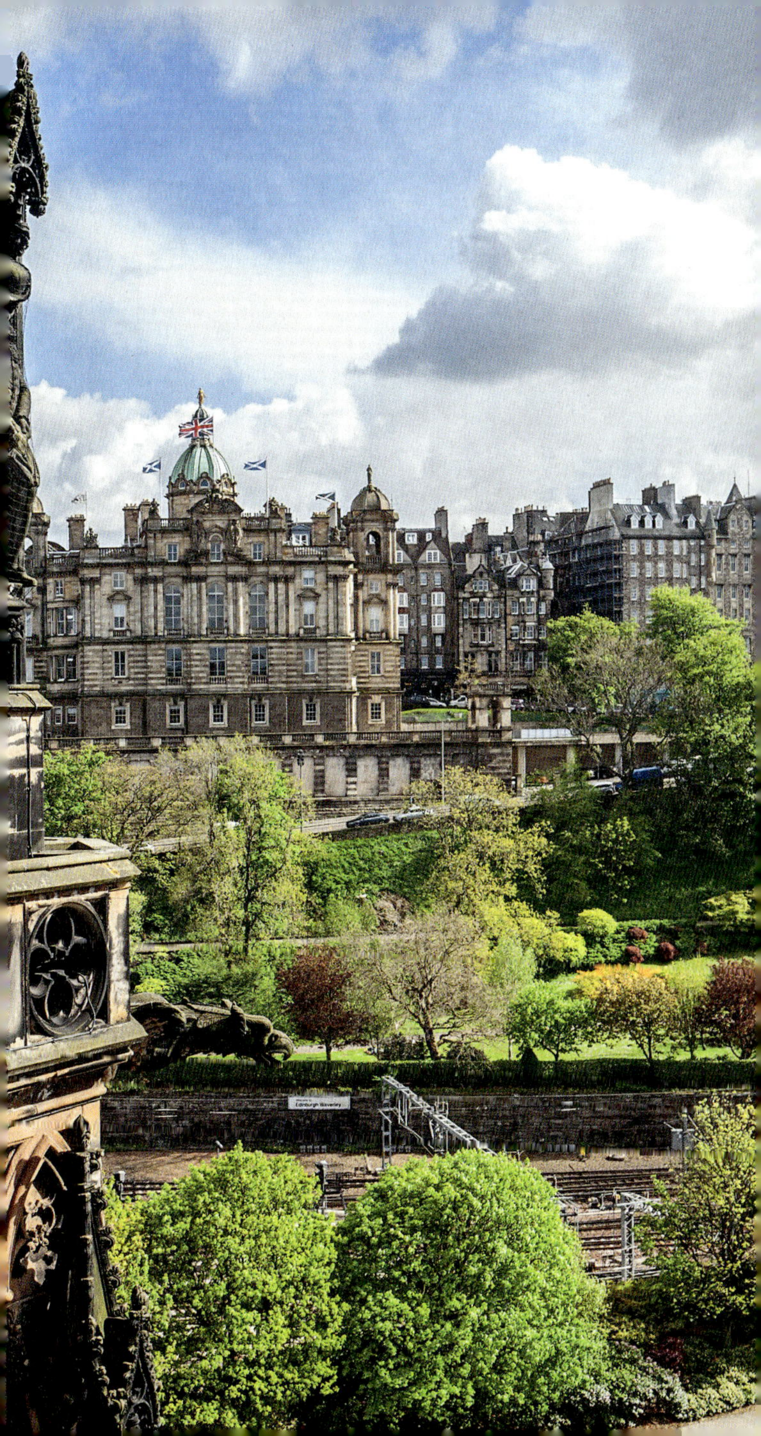

BEST ☂ WHEN IT RAINS

ACTIVITIES TO BRIGHTEN YOUR DAY

PLAY OF LIGHT IN THE CATHEDRAL
The play of light created by the stained-glass windows and modern glass screen behind the entrance at *St Giles' Cathedral* is impressive even in the rain. The chapel dedicated to an order of knights is home to two strange, carved angels playing bagpipes.
➤ p. 32, Sightseeing

HAUNTED WORLD BENEATH THE PAVEMENT
Beneath modern Edinburgh lies a warren of old, hidden lanes. *The Real Mary King's Close* attraction takes visitors underground for a tour that gives an authentic and gruesome impression of Edinburgh life from the 17th to 19th centuries.
➤ p. 33, Sightseeing

PREACHING & STORYTELLING
The Scots love telling stories. John Knox was a theologian and leader of the Scottish Reformation, and the opponent of Catholic queen Mary Stuart, known as Mary, Queen of Scots. Listen to the debates between the preacher and the queen in the fantastic Scottish Storytelling Centre in *John Knox House*. There's even a storytelling festival!
➤ p. 34, Sightseeing

NEOCLASSICAL TEMPLE OF THE ARTS
The neoclassical *Scottish National Gallery* exhibits world-famous works alongside Scottish highlights. It's worth visiting, if only to see Henry Raeburn's fabulous painting, *The Skating Minister*.
➤ p. 43, Sightseeing

WHAT A SHIP!
The *Royal Yacht Britannia*, with its Art Deco interior, is no longer in service and is now anchored at Leith. It's a sensory feast for the eyes (photo).
➤ p. 48, Sightseeing

BEST ON A BUDGET

FOR SMALLER WALLETS

FESTIVAL OF FESTIVALS
Once just an offshoot of the Edinburgh International Festival, the *Edinburgh Festival Fringe* is now an event in its own right; visitors arrive in droves to see comedy and theatre performances that don't cost the earth (photo).
➤ p. 18, Understand Edinburgh & p. 93, Festivals & events

DISCOVER THE CITY
The enthusiastic *edinburghfreetour.com* guides are devoted to their city, and know all about haunted houses and spitting, inventions, Scottish independence, and everything in between.
➤ p. 29, Sightseeing

SCOTLAND IN SESSION
The modern visionary construction of the *Scottish Parliament* fits perfectly into the Old Town. Satisfy your curiosity about its intriguing architecture on a free tour.
➤ p. 34, Sightseeing

MODERN ART FROM SCOTLAND'S CAPITAL
The *Scottish National Gallery of Modern Art Two* (next to Modern One) pays homage to Edinburgh's greatest artist, Eduardo Paolozzi – Surrealist, pop artist and sculptor – and admission is free!
➤ p. 47, Sightseeing

BEACH LIFE
A perfect spot to spend a sunny summer's day, *Portobello Beach* is a long stretch of golden sand, backed by a promenade with cafés, pubs and fish and chip shops.
➤ p. 49, Sightseeing

ALL ABOUT TARTAN
How do you shear a sheep? And how do you make a kilt from the wool? At the *Tartan Weaving Mill* you can find the answers and watch weavers at work, all for free.
➤ p. 74, Shopping

BEST WITH CHILDREN

FUN FOR YOUNG & OLD

TOYS OF THE PAST
What did children play with in decades gone by? What about your father's generation? Or his father's? Find out in the world's oldest *Museum of Childhood*.
➤ p. 34, Sightseeing

SHAKING EARTH & BUBBLING LAVA
What causes an earthquake? And a volcanic eruption? Science museum *Dynamic Earth* explains these aspects of geology under a huge canopy roof, directly next to Arthur's Seat, one of three extinct volcanoes in Edinburgh.
➤ p. 37, Sightseeing

INTERACTIVE MUSEUM
Kids get to have fun with interactive exhibits in the *National Museum of Scotland*. They can race against the road runner, launch hot-air balloons, present their fashion on a catwalk, see digital dinosaurs up close and get a robot to say their name.
➤ p. 38, Sightseeing

GET SCARED!
The ghost of Adam Lyal wanders through a gloomy Edinburgh. Rubbish is dropped into alleys from a great height, and everyone jumps in shock. We're back in the 17th century! Costumed actors and an Old Town backdrop make *horror tours* a great adventure for kids.
➤ p. 39, Sightseeing

TRAIN RIDE TO THE AQUARIUM
The *Deep Sea World* aquarium, with its rays and sharks, is not only a hit with kids – it's just as popular with older visitors, who love getting the train there across the famous red *Firth of Forth Bridge* (photo).
➤ p. 50, Sightseeing

10

BEST 🚩
CLASSIC EXPERIENCES

ONLY IN EDINBURGH

CASTLE ON THE ROCKS
Since it was built, *Edinburgh Castle* has dominated the city from its rocky perch. Enjoy the views and the Honours of Scotland crown jewels from up in the castle itself – or the silhouette of the volcanic rocks and lofty castle from below.
➤ p. 30, Sightseeing

A ROYAL PALACE
Feel the weight of Scotland's history as you tour the grand state apartments and throne room of the *Palace of Holyroodhouse*, one-time home to Mary, Queen of Scots and Bonnie Prince Charlie.
➤ p. 35, Sightseeing

MEMENTO MORI
Gloomy *Greyfriars Kirkyard* isn't just a graveyard: it's haunted. Notorious grave robbers Burke and Hare dug up bodies here to keep the city's anatomists supplied with cadavers for dissection.
➤ p. 39, Sightseeing

TIME FOR TEA
You too can drink tea from a bone-china cup and tuck into dainty sandwiches and scones in the hallowed halls of the famous *Signet Library*, one of Britain's finest Georgian buildings.
➤ p. 56, Eating & drinking

FARMERS' MARKET WITH A VIEW
The *Farmers' Market* at Edinburgh Castle opens at 9am on Saturdays. Farmers and environmentally conscious producers offer their exquisite produce for sale: wild boar, ostrich and water buffalo meat, organic beer, sourdough bread, honey, chutneys …
➤ p. 70, Shopping

FIDDLES IN THE BAR
A pint of bitter in your hand and melancholy dance rhythms in your ears: folk musicians come to jam at *Sandy Bell's* every day.
➤ p. 86, Nightlife

GET TO KNOW EDINBURGH

Shelter under an umbrella on the Royal Mile, but make sure it's tartan!

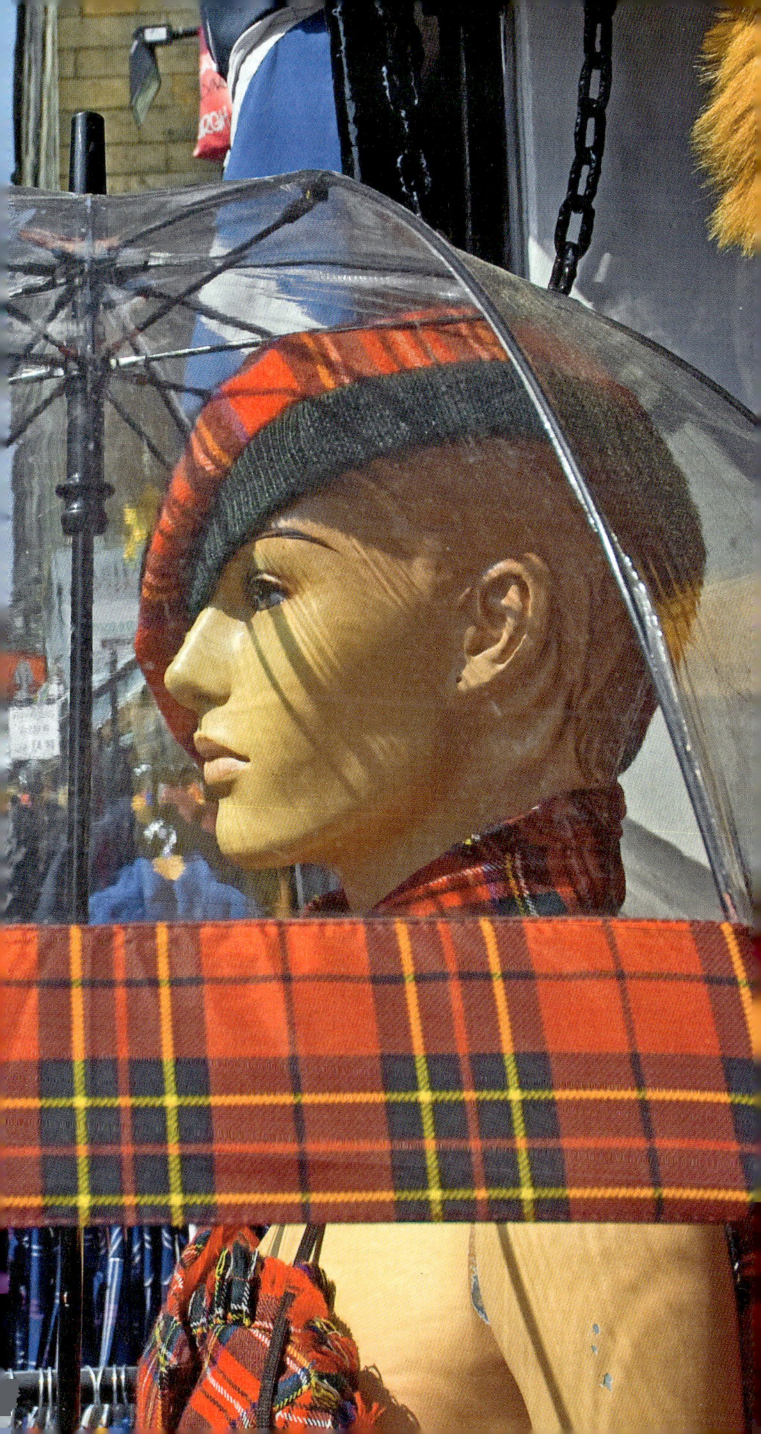

DISCOVER EDINBURGH

Around the Grassmarket buskers fill the air with their music

In terms of culture and history – and dynamism – Edinburgh has a lot to offer for its size. The verve and modernity of Edinburgh today – reflected in its festivals, for which it has become famous – is set against a backdrop of two historic towns located amid volcanic peaks that came together to form one unique capital.

AT THE FOOT OF THE CASTLE

Volcanic activity and ice ages left behind a rugged landscape on the estuary of the Firth of Forth, into which the compact metropolis is embedded. The castle, dating from the 12th century, and perched like an eyrie on a rocky hill, marked its beginnings, and the city developed at its base. The dramatic skyline of the Old Town at sunset creates an atmospheric portrait of the city, and is best viewed from Calton Hill.

731 Most northerly outpost of the Angles' kingdom of Northumbria

1093 The first mention of a castle here

around 1450 The first city wall is built, called the King's Wall

1505 The oldest society of surgeons in the world – the College of Surgeons – is founded here

1561 Mary, Queen of Scots arrives in Leith after 13 years in France

1707 Act of Union: Scotland joins Great Britain

GET TO KNOW EDINBURGH

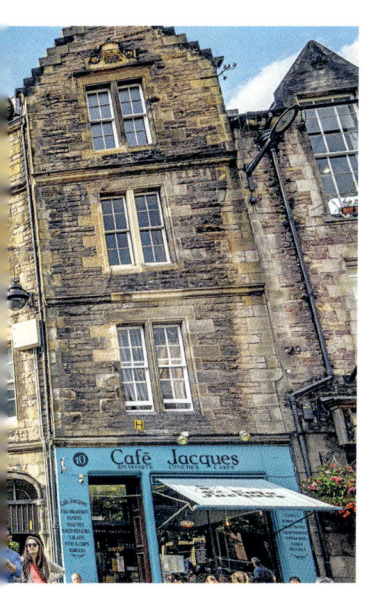

A NOVEL MAGNET
One man in particular is responsible for promoting the beautiful city of Edinburgh beyond the borders of Scotland. In the 19th century, author Walter Scott wove legends, with bloody battles against England and tragic love stories, into a series of historical novels. Meanwhile, other European writers felt that Edinburgh's dramatic geography and neoclassical architecture imbued it with the aura of an "Athens of the North". Scottish tourism, the *Highlander* film series and the *Outlander* TV series would be inconceivable without Scott. The same applies to the cult of the kilt. Scott turned the skirt-like piece of clothing worn by the Highlanders – and outlawed by the English – into a fashionable garment when he invited King George IV to Edinburgh in 1822 and gave him a kilt, which the king wore. The result: Scottish tartan became fashionable. In 2010, a new tartan was created for the Pope's visit and, in 2018, Burberry released a rainbow tartan for the LGBT+ community.

INTELLECTUAL HEIGHTS AND A STINKING CITY
Scotland was bankrupt at the beginning of the 18th century, but in 1708 it was united with England in the Act of Union and governed from London. The result was an economic boom and promotion of the country's talent. The Scottish Enlightenment brought new scientific and intellectual heights: the first faculty of medicine in Britain was established in Edinburgh in 1726, followed by a philosophical society in 1739. Adam Smith, the father of economic theory, was

1767–1835 New Town is built and expanded

1947 The first Edinburgh International Festival and Fringe Festival

1997 Scottish scientists clone Dolly the sheep

2016 74.3% of Edinburgh votes against Brexit, 62% of Scotland votes against Brexit

2023 Nicola Sturgeon steps back as first minister; her successor Humza Yousaf resigns in 2024, and is replaced by John Swinney; tram expanded to reach Leith and Newhaven

from Edinburgh – in the opinion of many, including Voltaire, the city had suddenly become Europe's main intellectual centre.

At the same time as this intellectual flourishing, around 50,000 inhabitants lived in cramped conditions in 12-storey buildings in the Old Town. The well-to-do citizens lived in the lower storeys, with the poorer souls above. The place stank thanks to all the residents' slops being tipped out of windows into the alley below – called a close or a *wynd* – at bedtime. If you threw your tankard at the wall of a pub, it is said that it would stick to the filth on the wall. In spite of this, new ideas formed in these pubs.

From Calton Hill or the colossal memorial for Walter Scott, you can see how the city developed along lines influenced by the Enlightenment: on the left, you will see the Middle Ages, with the old castle sweeping down from the hilltop to the Palace of Holyroodhouse; on the right, a completely different city comes into view – the Georgian New Town, built from around 1770, represents the zenith of city planning of the period: uniform, precise and spacious. In response to the overcrowding in the Old Town, this other half of Edinburgh was created south of Nor Loch, a heavily polluted body of water in which witches had once been drowned. This drained lake is today the green heartland of Edinburgh: Princes Street Gardens. The architectural triumph of the New Town is an important piece of cultural heritage. It is fairly easy to explore both the Old Town and New Town on foot, but expect hills, steps and rough cobblestones.

THE SCOTTISH SOUL OF EDINBURGH

Today, Edinburgh is Scotland's second-largest city. The largest, Glasgow (only 50 minutes away by train), is less touristy and with a greater working-class heritage. Edinburgh is considered more middle class, with civil servants from the Scottish government walking around in suits and ties. Four-fifths of all Scots voted in favour of devolution in 1997, and the newly created Scottish Parliament moved into its new residence in Edinburgh in 2004. Designed by Catalan architect Enric Miralles, the Parliament Building made quite a statement.

And now? Scotland often finds itself juxtaposed politically with London in terms of social issues, education and the environment. While Scottish people voted to remain part of Britain in the 2014 independence referendum, two-thirds of Scots voted to remain in Europe in the 2016 Brexit referendum, adding new vigour to the issue of Scottish independence. However, after scandals and leadership changes within the party, the issue seems to be on the back burner for the moment. In addition, in 2022 the UK Supreme Court ruled that the Scottish Government does not have the necessary powers to legislate for a second referendum.

While Scotland's future may remain in doubt, what is certain is that the country today is forward-looking and progressive. Edinburgh has opened itself to the world through its annual festivals, which attract international talent. But even outside festival season, Edinburgh is a city ready to welcome visitors.

GET TO KNOW EDINBURGH

AT A GLANCE

554,000
inhabitants

Greater London: 8.9 million

190
Days of rain per year

Number of pubs in the city: 385

264km²
area

London: 1,572km²

OFFICIAL LANGUAGES

3

English, Scots, Scottish Gaelic

FESTIVAL VISITORS

4.7 million PER YEAR

MOST POPULAR MONTH TO VISIT

AUGUST

VOLCANOES IN THE CITY

The three hills in the centre of Edinburgh have volcanic origins; the highest point is the extinct volcano Arthur's Seat (250m)

TOP PLACES

1. National Museum of Scotland
2. Edinburgh Castle

MOST FAMOUS PEOPLE:

MARY STUART
ALEXANDER FLEMING
SEAN CONNERY

UNDERSTAND EDINBURGH

THAT JEKYLL & HYDE FEELING

Horror and glamour, Old Town and New Town – these contrasts complement each other in the most exciting ways in Edinburgh. On one side are the narrow alleys and winding streets of the medieval Old Town, set between two volcanic hills; on the other the fine neoclassical lines of the New Town. This is a cityscape with a split personality – a Jekyll and Hyde city (don't forget their creator, Robert Louis Stevenson, was a son of Edinburgh – his former home is now a hotel).

Scary walking tours and the 3D effects of a digital cadaver in the *Surgeons' Hall Museums* convincingly conjure up a horrifying Edinburgh, one where the body thieves and murderers Burke and Hare lurked. It may also lead you underground, if you descend into the excellent re-enactment of 17th-century Edinburgh at *The Real Mary King's Close*.

DANGEROUS PIPES

Bagpipes create a distinctive and melancholy soundtrack for Edinburgh. There have been strong differences of opinion about the sounds that come out of these squawking bags. After the final battle for Scotland in Culloden in 1746, piper James Reid was sentenced to death because the court martial classified his bagpipes as a weapon of war. This led to the rumour that the English would impose the death penalty on anybody playing the pipes. This was not the case. However, the debate over the pipes continued. One piper in London had to pay a fine for making too much noise, although the court refused to accept that the death penalty imposed on James Reid could be taken as a precedent, instead ruling that the bagpipe was indeed a musical instrument.

A CITY CELEBRATES

Every year, Edinburgh hosts dozens of festivals. Viennese emigrant Sir Rudolf Bing initiated the now world-famous ★ *Edinburgh International Festival (EIF)* (see p. 93) as a platform for the arts in 1947. Music, the sciences, pagan-Celtic customs and the art of storytelling are all focuses for festivals here. In the month of August, the population of the capital doubles, as the EIF, the Edinburgh International Book Festival, Military Tattoo and, most importantly, the huge ★ *Edinburgh Festival Fringe* (see p. 93) all take place at the same time.

At the Fringe, quirky theatre and alternative comedy takes place in pubs and other small venues, while serious plays fill the larger stages; but you'll also find cabaret, dance, music, spoken word, exhibitions and other events. At the same time, legions of street artists juggle and tumble through the alleyways. Today, the Fringe is the largest performing arts festival in the world.

GET TO KNOW EDINBURGH

The perfect souvenir: Scotland's soul can be found in a single swig of whisky

DRUNK ON WHISKY

The ancient Celts called their drink *uisge beatha*, the "water of life", which was subsequently shortened to *whisky*. The first written record of the drink appeared in 1494, when a certain John Cor ordered a ton of malt to make "aqua vitae". The Scottish government looked to profit from whisky's popularity and introduced taxes in 1644, leading to illicit stills popping up everywhere, and smuggling became a way of life in Scotland. In 1823, the Excise Act sanctioned the distilling of whisky in return for a licence fee, and smuggling began to die out.

During the 19th century, entrepreneurs like Tommy Dewar, Johnnie Walker and James Chivas took whisky out of Scotland to a wider market. Single malt whisky is now a hallmark of the country, even though single malts only account for approximately ten per cent of all whisky sold. The drink, with its layers of tasting notes, is reinvented time and again, and the names of the whiskies range from classic to whacky, alongside sober mentions on the label of the distillery and age. Glenfiddich is one of the best-known everyday offerings of single malts. Poit Dhubh is a blended malt, its poetic-sounding Gaelic name reminiscent of an old, illegal distillery. Blended malts are several single malts from different distilleries combined by experts. But don't confuse them with blended whisky, which consists of a single malt made with malted barley, mixed with grain whiskies that can be made with a variety of grains.

The Royal Edinburgh Military Tattoo is an impressive event

You can get all types of whisky in Edinburgh and, since 2023, there is even a distillery in a tower on the firth in Leith. It's a booming market: new distilleries are appearing all over the place, but you'll have to wait to taste a newcomer's product, as the drink has to be stored for at least three years to be called whisky.

SONS OF SCOTLAND

Former British prime minister Tony Blair was born in Edinburgh, and attended its famous Fettes College. And he's not the city's only famous son. As a child, Sean Connery worked delivering milk to Fettes College in a pony-driven cart, and as a lifeguard at Portobello Beach; he was even Mr Scotland in the Mr Universe competition (where he achieved third place). Of course, Connery is best known for his role as James Bond and, coincidentally, Ian Fleming made his fictional hero an alumnus of Fettes College. Connery was a supporter of the Scottish National Party. He died in October 2020, at the age of 90.

Other less high-profile but just as important figures from Edinburgh include John Boyd Dunlop, inventor of air-filled tyres; waterproof clothing was invented by Charles Mackintosh; Alexander Graham Bell brought the first telephone to market by ousting a competitor; and Annie Lennox is the very cool music icon of the 1980s …

GET TO KNOW EDINBURGH

THE DARK SIDE
Edinburgh also harbours a darker, colder side to its personality, which has been reflected in fiction. Ian Rankin sent out his Detective Inspector Rebus to solve crimes in and around the city, and Robert Louis Stevenson created the character of Dr Jekyll, who transforms into the murderous Mr Hyde in *The Strange Case of Dr Jekyll and Mr Hyde*. Meanwhile, Irvine Welsh's novel *Trainspotting*, which was turned into a film by Danny Boyle, highlights poverty in Edinburgh and is full of morally ambiguous and less than virtuous characters. (Incidentally, although the film is set in Edinburgh it was mainly filmed in Glasgow.)

TARTAN & THE KILT
The word *tartan* comes from Gaelic, while *kilt* is said to derive from Old Norse. The modern kilt originates from traditional Highland male dress from the 16th century, probably emerging in the form we see today during the 18th century. The kilt was actually banned in 1746, as part of an English move to suppress Highland culture. It fell out of use after that, but became associated with romantic nostalgia for the rugged, "simple" life of the Highlanders. Once the ban was lifted in 1782, landowners set up Highland Societies, which, among other things, promoted "the use of the ancient Highland dress". And the Royal Celtic Society, headed by novelist Walter Scott, encouraged lowlanders to take up the kilt too, as a symbol of Scottishness. Scott even put George IV in a kilt when he visited

TRUE OR FALSE?

HAUNTED ON EVERY CORNER
Edinburgh has horror in its blood. Bodies were dug up and people were murdered to provide cadavers for anatomical research. Witches were drowned in the Nor Loch – now the innocent grassy park of Princes Street Gardens. In *The Strange Case of Dr Jekyll and Mr Hyde*, Robert Louis Stevenson described a horrifying double life. Nonetheless, the city has lots of light to offer, especially when the festivals arrive and people party like crazy.

COLD & RAINY
Brrrr, Edinburgh is often wet and windy. On the edge of the North Atlantic, Edinburgh's weather is unpredictable and the winds can be strong. But during the summer months it can be warm, so watch out for sunburn. In the winter, the sun often shines so low down in the sky that it can dazzle you all day long.

TOO STEEP TO CYCLE!
Thinking of cycling around the city? While the hills and sloping cobbled streets aren't that enticing, there is still a lovely series of cycle paths throughout the flat, green parts of the city. See also p. 90

Edinburgh in 1822, after which its popularity took off. Today, Scottish men often attend weddings in a – usually rented – kilt.

It takes around three by six metres of woollen fabric to make a kilt; the pattern of the tartan used is determined by the clan the wearer belongs to. Today, the likes of Amnesty International, the royal family, the Pope, and even the LGBT+ community, have their own tartans. The kilt is worn with knee-high socks, and a small knife, the *sgian dubh*, is traditionally tucked into the side of the socks. The question of what is worn under the kilt remains known only to the Scots.

DEVOLUTION & BEYOND

Tony Blair's devolution policy meant that Edinburgh got its own parliament in 1999, for the first time since the 1707 Act of Union. However, Scotland still elects MPs for the UK Parliament in Westminster, and the powers of the Scottish Parliament are limited to issues pertaining to Scotland only. Other issues are "reserved" for the UK Parliament.

The Scottish National Party (SNP) is currently in power. Its leading policy is independence from Britain, but it failed to secure a majority for this in a 2014 referendum. The independence issue became particularly hot when the Scots were forced to accept Brexit, despite voting against it by a wide margin, in the 2016 referendum. Brexit certainly shook the cohesion of Britain in the long term but, after a swing against the SNP in the 2024 UK general election, it is unclear whether

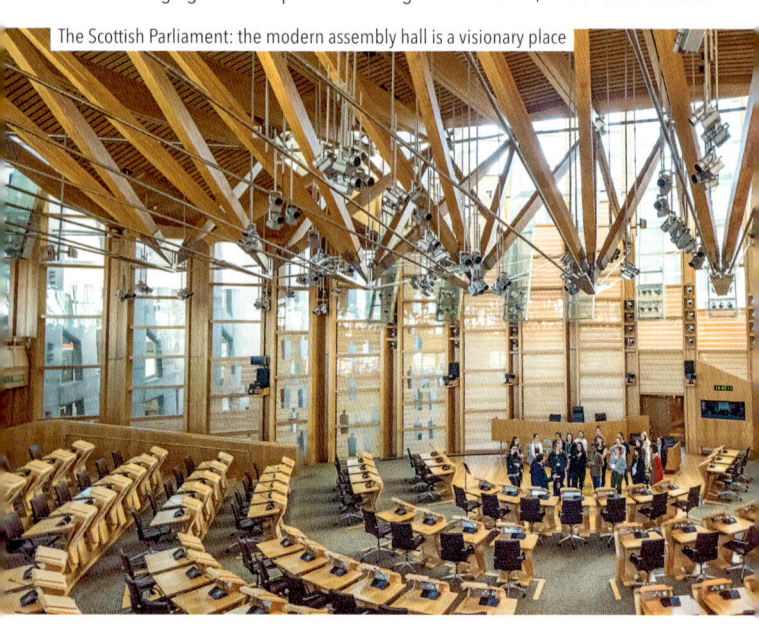

The Scottish Parliament: the modern assembly hall is a visionary place

GET TO KNOW EDINBURGH

the tug of war for Scottish independence will continue.

MARY, QUEEN OF SCOTS

Mary Stuart was a beauty, with manners learnt at the French royal court, where she lived from 1548 until her return to Leith as a young widow. She became the Queen of Scots in 1542, when she was just six days old, on the death of her father. She returned in 1561 to an Edinburgh embroiled in the tense religious and political climate of the Scottish Reformation. The fun-loving girl with a penchant for golf was Catholic, which drove her arch enemy and Edinburgh neighbour, the reformer John Knox, to preach angry sermons against her and her beliefs in St Giles' Cathedral. You can listen to how the two of them argued in re-enacted dialogues in John Knox House (p. 34).

Political wranglings cost Mary the throne in 1567, and she was imprisoned in England. Her protestant cousin, Queen Elizabeth I, left her there for 19 years, before beheading her in 1587.

SCOTS VERSUS ENGLISH

Scotland officially has three languages: English, Scots and Gaelic. English is the official spoken language in Edinburgh. However, many inject Scots – arguably more of a dialect than a language – into their choice of words and pronunciation. The two languages are closely related and often mixed together. Some Scots words, like "bairn", "wee" and "kirk", are familiar to many UK English speakers. Other words will be less familiar. For example, "scunnered" means fed up, and "glaikit" means stupid.

Scots was the official language of Scotland until 1707. You can still hear a lot of Scots being spoken in pubs and shops around Edinburgh. As an oral language, it's spelled the way it sounds. If you're interested in finding out more, browse through a novel by Irvine Welsh. *Trainspotting* (1997) is written in Scots. Edinburgh's old nickname *Auld Reekie* (Old Smokey) comes from Scots, as do the names of the alleyways along the Royal Mile: *close* (courtyard entrance) and *wynd* (alleyway between two streets). In Glasgow, the accent and dialect are more influenced by Irish and Highland speech – it really does sound different.

SIGHT SEEING

Edinburgh looks more like a theatre set than a modern metropolis. Climb one of the three steep volcanic hills in the centre and you will see two historic urban centres at your feet – one medieval, the other dating from the 18th and 19th centuries – but hardly any modern architecture. The Old Town and New Town that create the city of Edinburgh are together a UNESCO World Heritage Site.

Seen from Edinburgh Castle or Arthur's Seat, you won't be surprised that the urban drama that unfolds below has inspired writers

> You'll find all the venues in this chapter on the pull-out map

Royal Mile: the heart of the Old Town

for three centuries. Descend to this splendid real-life theatre, and you'll find that everything is within easy strolling distance – and there is no need to rush. After all, you don't want to miss anything.

Edinburgh has many intimate corners where you can stop and feel what lies beneath the city's surface. So don't overlook any alleyways, flights of steps, or cemeteries, and grasp every opportunity to have a chat with the locals. At the eastern end of the Old Town, the historic meets the modern with the architectural masterpiece that is the Scottish Parliament Building.

REGIONAL OVERVIEW

MARCO POLO HIGHLIGHTS

★ **ROYAL MILE**
Feel the city's heartbeat on the iconic street between the castle and the palace ➤ p. 28

★ **EDINBURGH CASTLE**
Scotland's mightiest royal castle rises high above the city on a volcanic rock ➤ p. 30

★ **SCOTTISH PARLIAMENT**
The building for Scotland's new millennium was inserted ingeniously into the Old Town ➤ p. 34

★ **SURGEONS' HALL MUSEUMS**
Anatomy at its most fascinating. Learn more about surgery through time – it might give you goosebumps ➤ p. 38

★ **NATIONAL MUSEUM OF SCOTLAND**
Enjoy the historic, modern and diverse in these magnificent rooms – the best of Scotland! ➤ p. 38

★ **PRINCES STREET GARDENS**
Edinburgh's answer to New York's Central Park is a green valley in the heart of the city, with a view up to the Old Town ➤ p. 42

★ **CALTON HILL**
The volcanic hill is like a painting; perfect for romantic evening views of the city ➤ p. 44

★ **SCOTTISH NATIONAL GALLERY OF MODERN ART**
Two impressive neoclassical temples for modern art ➤ p. 47

★ **ROYAL YACHT BRITANNIA**
Queen Elizabeth II's yacht is now in retirement and open for visitors ➤ p. 48

★ **ROYAL BOTANIC GARDEN**
Wonderfully tamed wilderness dating from the 17th century, with plants from all over the world ➤ p. 48

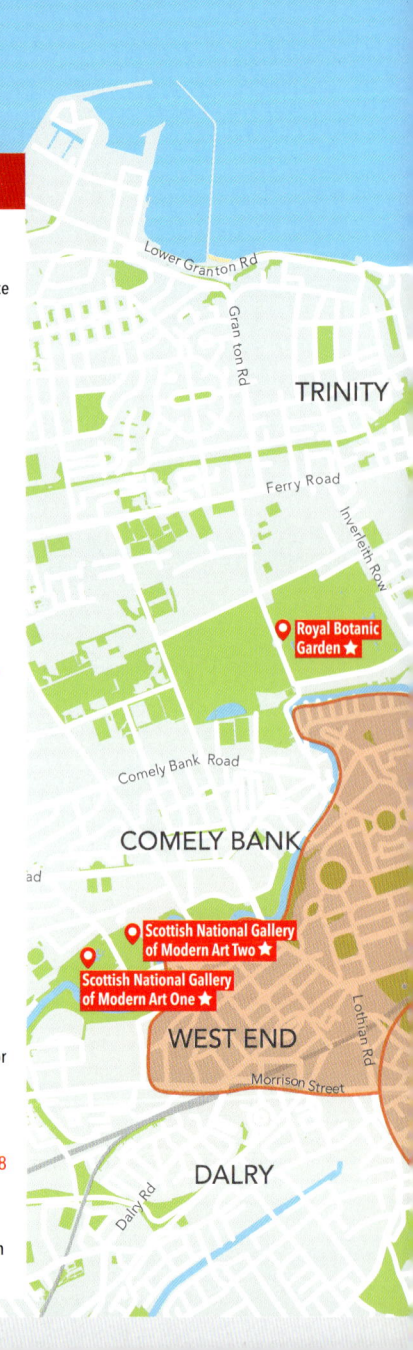

Map of Edinburgh

Areas & Neighborhoods: NEWHAVEN, LEITH, WARRISTON, BROUGHTON, ABBEYHILL, SOUTHSIDE, NEWINGTON

NEW TOWN p. 40
Elegance and spaciousness: revel in the Georgian architecture

OLD TOWN p. 28
Medieval alleyways and the Royal Mile, in the shadow of the mighty castle

Points of Interest
- Royal Yacht Britannia ★
- Calton Hill ★
- Scottish Parliament ★
- Royal Mile ★
- Princes Street Gardens ★
- Surgeons' Hall Museums ★
- National Museum of Scotland ★
- Edinburgh Castle ★

Streets
Lindsay Rd, Craighall Rd, Commercial St, Salamander St, Constitution, Easter Rd, Lochend Rd, Restalrig Rd, Leith Walk, Broughton Road, Eyre Place, Bellevue, Elm Row, London Road, Queen St, Leith St, Regent Rd, Princes St, Holyrood Rd, Dalkeith Road, Clerk St, Melville Drive

Other
Holyrood Park

500 m / 547 yd

OLD TOWN

> ### WHERE TO START?
>
> It's easy to explore both the Old and New Towns on foot if you start at **Waverley Station** *(F4)*. A flight of steps leads to the Royal Mile, where Edinburgh Castle, the Scottish Parliament and the Palace of Holyroodhouse can be found. The elegant shops on George Street and St Andrew Square in the New Town are also only a five-minute walk from Waverley. Parking: underground car park at Waverley Station, New Street. From the airport: a tram runs every ten minutes to Princes Street and the train station (35 mins, £7.50).

OLD TOWN

The Royal Mile is where you will feel the true heartbeat of Edinburgh – all the way along its entire length of almost 1.8km, the equivalent of an old Scottish mile.

The Royal Mile runs all the way from the castle to the Palace of Holyroodhouse, and you can easily spend a day strolling here. Shops on the ground floor of the old buildings, with their kilts, tartans and whisky, tend towards the kitsch. But you will also discover small restaurants and cafés, churches, museums and lanes with steps that branch off the Mile like ribs from the backbone.

To the south, the streets appear more like canyons – narrow lanes lined with high buildings. Small, steep connecting lanes such as *Victoria Street*, *Candlemaker Row* and *King's Stables Road* lead like arteries to the lively heart of the Old Town. There, any number of boutiques flourish between tap rooms, coffee-houses and restaurants. And a pulsating nightlife can be found in the medieval labyrinth of streets between the *Grassmarket*, *Cowgate* and *Nicholson Street*. The streets in the Old Town are often short and steep, but you don't need a bus to get around.

Edinburgh is an attractive city, especially the New Town, which seems to consciously show off its unique architectural splendour. Walk through the gorgeous Princes Street Gardens on your way to this fascinating Georgian half of the city, whose construction began in the late 18th century. Robert Louis Stevenson grew up here and he immortalised the hybrid nature of his hometown in his novel about the good-natured Dr Jekyll who turned into the murderous Mr Hyde. For the finale of your Edinburgh exploration, head west. You can walk – or even better, cycle – along the small river called the Water of Leith through a charming rural area that runs down to the old port of Leith, which has now developed into a popular eating and entertainment hub, with Michelin-star restaurants.

1 ROYAL MILE ★

It is said that around 50,000 people lived on the Royal Mile and the streets branching off of it – the *closes* and *wynds* – in the 18th century; the highest population density per square

SIGHTSEEING

metre in Europe at the time. The residential buildings, the *lands*, had as many as 12 storeys; the poor lived at the bottom and top while the better-off merchants, craftsmen and lawyers had their flats in between. The well-trodden sets of steps on each side of the Mile can lead to picturesque courtyards – it is worth following them from time to time. Or you might unexpectedly find your way over the threshold of a hidden pub and soon get chatting with the locals at the bar over a glass of real ale. Keep an eye open for guided ghost tours. Luckily, the city's ultimate horror has been done away with: today, nobody has to take cover when the bell of St Giles' Cathedral chimes ten o'clock, followed by the warning cry of *"gardy luh"* (from the French *"gardez l'eau"* – watch out, water!) – when the contents of all the chamber pots were emptied into the streets. Especially in the upper half, the Mile is a succession of little shops stuffed with Scotch kitsch. Its centrepiece is the main church, *St Giles' Cathedral*, with its chapel from the Order of the Thistle.

The Royal Mile is roughly divided into four sections: *Castle Hill*, *Lawnmarket*, *High Street* and *Canongate*. Lawnmarket boasts a monument to the famous Edinburgh philosopher and economist David Hume (1711–76), a friend of the economist Adam Smith. *Free tours* through the city start every day at 10am, 11am and 1pm from the High Street at the *Tron Kirk (edinburghfreetour.com)*.

A holy highlight on the Royal Mile: St Giles' Cathedral

OLD TOWN

For many years, Canongate lay outside the city boundary, separated by the *Flodden Wall*; you can still see traces of this in the tarmac on the street between Greyfriars and the National Museum *(corner of Chambers Street/Forrest Road)*. There is a statue of the poet Robert Fergusson (1750–74), who died young, in front of the small *Canongate Kirk* in the Canongate section (members of the royal family attend services here when they are at the palace). Not far from the parliament, you can see sculptor David Annand's statue of poet Robert Fergusson in full stride (see p. 119). When it was unveiled in 2004, an actor dressed up as Robert Burns leapt out of the crowd and recited some of Fergusson's verses. You will also find Fergusson's grave (he died at the age of 24) in *Canongate Cemetery*, along with those of economist Adam Smith and Mary, Queen of Scots' murdered secretary, David Rizzio. Robert Burns was greatly inspired by Fergusson's work, and donated the poet's headstone (later renovated by Robert Louis Stevenson).
 e–h 4–5

2 EDINBURGH CASTLE ★

This castle is set high above the city on a volcanic hill. Castle Hill slopes steeply downwards on three sides but the Old Town finds its way gently into the valley on its eastern flank.

It is difficult to imagine just how remote this castle must have looked in the 7th century when King Edwin of Northumbria in the northeast of England had a lonely fortress erected here. Later, kings were fathered and born here, prisoners locked in the dungeons and guests assassinated.

The two freedom fighters William Wallace (1270–1305) and King Robert the Bruce (1274–1329) have taken up position at the entrance, the *Gatehouse,* built in 1887. In summer, it is hard to get a good look at them with so many other visitors behind you pushing to get in. Shortly after passing the bottleneck at the *Portcullis Gate*, you will find yourself standing in front of the castle's two main attractions. First, the enormous Mons Meg Cannon – probably made in Mons, Belgium in 1457. It weights 6 tonnes and could shoot stone cannonballs

Edinburgh Castle will attract your attention from all sides

SIGHTSEEING

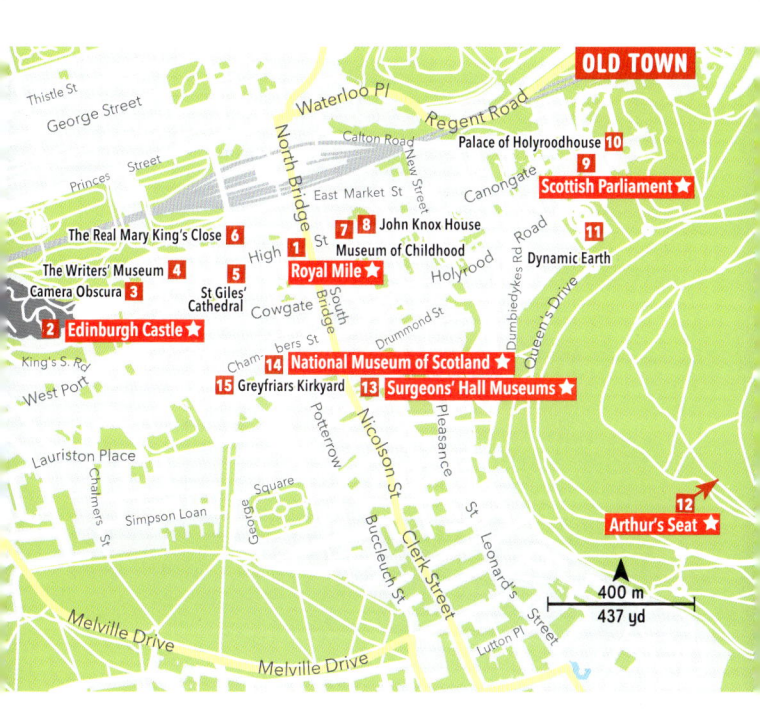

with a diameter of 50cm weighing 150kg. It was fired for the last time in 1681. Today, a modern 105mm weapon lets off a shot Monday to Saturday at 1pm. People in the city call this the "lunchtime bang". In the 19th century, sailors in the port outside the city used this to adjust their chronometers, so the shot needed to be loud.

The other highlight is *St Margaret's Chapel* from the 12th century. It was possibly built by King David I in memory of his mother Margaret, a Scottish queen who was canonised for her social commitment. The unpretentious chapel in Norman style with a slightly asymmetrical layout is the oldest building in Edinburgh.

The Scottish crown jewels (16th century) – the crown, created by James Mossmann (*John Knox House,* see p. 34), the sceptre and sword – are on display in the Crown Hall under the title *Honours of Scotland*. In 1996, they were joined by an even older – and, for Scots, much more important – ancient artefact, the *Stone of Scone* (pronounced *scoon*). The stone was used in the coronation of the early kings of the Scots and Picts, until the English seized it in 1296 and placed it under the English Coronation Chair. It was returned 700 years later in a ceremony shortly before Scotland voted in favour of devolution.

The rest of the castle is made up of a few barracks buildings but what's truly impressive is the fantastic view over

31

OLD TOWN

the city and surrounding countryside.

> **INSIDER TIP: Online tickets**
> Online tickets are slightly cheaper and allow you to get in more quickly.

Daily April–Sept 9.30am–6pm, Oct–March 9.30am–5pm | admission £15.50 (online) | Castlehill | edinburghcastle.scot | ⏱ from 1 hr | 🗺 d–e5

3 CAMERA OBSCURA ☂

It fascinated Victorian tourists from 1853 and continues to intrigue visitors today. A kind of pinhole camera with a focal length of 8.6m projects views of Edinburgh into the dark upper storey of a tower next to the castle. As if by magic, images of sections of the city appear before the visitors' eyes in the tower room. Five floors are packed with various illusions, that there are also stupendous real views from the rooftop.

Interactive exhibits explain visual phenomena such as holograms and plasma-energy. The Camera Obscura is more interesting when the weather is fine, but the exhibitions will also help you forget a rainy day. *Daily April–June 9.30am–8pm, July/Aug 9am–10pm, Sept/Oct 9.30am–8pm, Nov–March Mon-Fri 10am–7pm, Sat until 10am–9pm | admission £19.95 | 549 Castlehill | camera-obscura.co.uk | ⏱ 45–90 mins | 🗺 e5*

4 THE WRITERS' MUSEUM 🐗

A magnet for book lovers! This building from 1622 is the only original house in the street leading off the *Lawnmarket* section of the Royal Mile. Today, it is a museum commemorating the writing trio Burns, Scott and Stevenson. Early editions of their works are on display, along with personal mementos including Burns' snuffbox. There's also a cosy reading corner. Sometimes exhibitions focus on the work of modern writers. *Daily 10am–5pm | free admission | Lady Stair's Close, Lawnmarket, Royal Mile | edinburghmuseums.org.uk | ⏱ 1 hr | 🗺 f5*

5 ST GILES' CATHEDRAL ☂

St Giles doesn't seem very inviting at first glance. The building is almost lost on the Royal Mile and you could possibly even walk past it if it were not for the boldly playful tower in the shape of a crown. Its real name is the *High Kirk of St Giles*, and it is a Church of Scotland church that worships in the Scottish Presbyterian tradition. So it is not actually a cathedral. The Church of Scotland has a democratic assembly of Presbyters (elders) instead of a strict hierarchy.

Church services have been held on this site since 854, although the pillars around the altar from 1120 are now the oldest surviving remains of the current building. The new building was erected in the Gothic style after its predecessor had been destroyed by the English. The severe Gothic dimensions must have pleased Calvinist reformer John Knox: it provided the perfect stage for the blazing sermons he delivered here from 1560 to 1572. St Giles was hardly quiet later on either. Edinburgh's church history is characterised by countless intellectual

SIGHTSEEING

conflicts over the true faith. The tours that take place every day are very worthwhile.

The fascinating *Chapel of the Scottish Order of the Thistle*, built in 1911, is a real gem, with its exquisite wood and stone carving. The national emblem of Scotland in the order's name – it's the second highest British honour after the Order of the Garter – is a clear indication that the 16 knights, men and women, who are members at any one time, must be Scottish. The sovereign and various "extra knights", currently Queen Camilla, Prince William and Princess Anne, are also considered to be members.

Each knight has their own seat, decorated with their coat of arms, in the church's oak stalls – commoners have to have one designed before they can be admitted to the order. David Steel, the first Presiding Officer of the Scottish Parliament, had a jaguar added to his coat of arms; some people felt this was because he was so fond of the car of the same name. To see the most unusual decorations in the chapel, you have to look up: the arched ceiling includes two angels – playing bagpipes, of course. *Tue–Fri 10am–6pm, Sat 9am–5pm, Sun 1–5pm | free admission | Lawnmarket, Royal Mile | stgilescathedral.org.uk |* 1–2 hrs | f5

INSIDER TIP: Musical angels

6 THE REAL MARY KING'S CLOSE

Discover life in the 17th century on this (haunted) underground street.

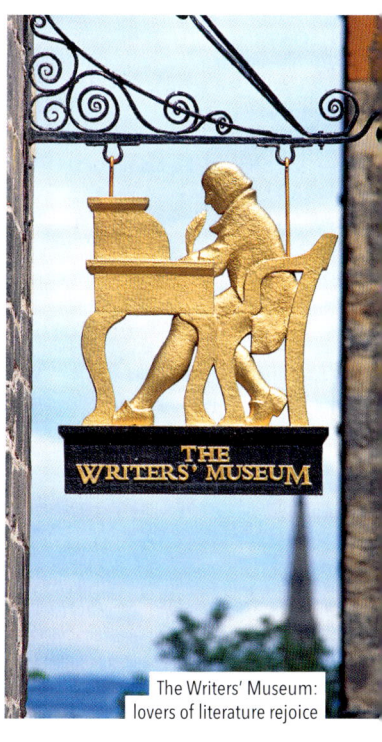

The Writers' Museum: lovers of literature rejoice

New buildings were constructed on top of an old labyrinth of small streets next to the Royal Mile. The underground site was reopened as a tourist attraction in 1996. Its reputation as a haunted close likely originated from the eerie gases that escaped into the close from the stagnant and highly polluted marsh Nor Loch, nearby (today Princes Street Gardens). The reputation was intensified by the stories of hauntings of plague victims quarantined in the close. A visit to the close (online booking strongly recommended and arrive 15 minutes before the tour) lets you explore medieval hauntings in Edinburgh.

33

OLD TOWN

Mid-March–Oct Mon–Thu 10am–5pm, Fri–Sun 9.30am–7pm, Nov–mid-March Sun–Thu 10am–5.30pm, Fri, Sat 10am–9pm | admission from £21 | 2 Warriston's Close/High Street | realmarykingsclose.com | ⏱ 1 hr | 📖 f5

7 MUSEUM OF CHILDHOOD
Parents and their children immerse themselves in the history of childhood and discover what kids played with before the advent of the smartphone. Wonderful exhibits in the world's first childhood museum, renovated in 2018, show how kids used to live in Edinburgh. *Daily 10am–5pm | free admission | 42 High Street | edinburghmuseums.org.uk | ⏱ 1 hr | 📖 g5*

8 JOHN KNOX HOUSE
This 500-year-old house is definitely the most homely building on the Royal Mile. John Knox, the founder of Scottish Presbyterianism, may possibly have lived in the building and this saved it from demolition in 1830. Knox was inspired by religious reformer John Calvin in Geneva, and set out to reform Scotland's church. What is certain, however, is that Knox's contemporary, wealthy goldsmith James Mossmann, who was responsible for the Scottish crown, actually did live here. He safeguarded his home by having an entrance on the first floor, stairs that are difficult to negotiate and false locks.

You enter the rooms via a spiral staircase. The faded original ceiling paintings and furniture from the Knox and Mossmann era lend an authentic atmosphere. While you look out of the window at what is happening on the Royal Mile, you will suddenly hear debates between Knox and Mossmann or Mary, Queen of Scots. The Catholic Queen of Scotland, who had been educated in France, and the strict, quarrelsome religious teacher often clashed with each other – Knox disapproved of her lifestyle as well as her theology. It should be noted that the church reformer and father of several daughters was generally suspicious of women, as shown by his treatise, *The First Blast of the Trumpet against the Monstrous Regiment of Women*, which is on display.

John Knox was considered a charismatic speaker. The Scottish Storytelling Centre attached to the John Knox House focuses on the skill of rhetoric and the typical Scottish pleasure in telling tales. There is an interactive "Scotland's Stories" exhibition in the cheerful rooms, and a pleasant café. ==Funny, sad and dramatic stories are told "eye to eye, heart to heart" in a theatre with a capacity for 99 people.== **INSIDER TIP: Tell me a story** In October the International Storytelling Festival is held here. *Daily 10am–6pm | admission £5, Storytelling Centre free | 43 High Street | scottishstorytellingcentre.com/john-knox-house | ⏱ 1 hr | 📖 g5*

9 SCOTTISH PARLIAMENT ⭐
An exciting contrast in building styles awaits you at the lower end of the Royal Mile. In the parliament building, internationally renowned Catalan architect Enric Miralles demonstrated

SIGHTSEEING

A stained-glass window depicting reformer John Knox

how a modern structure could find its place amid narrow lanes and clusters of houses, many of which had been built centuries ago. Most people interpret the building's design as inspired by the geography of the Old Town and the topography of Scotland. However, the architect died at the age of 45, before construction was completed in 2004, and so was not able to explain some of the puzzling features of the building, such as the scale-like design of the rear windows and the shape of the seats.

A 1685 building *(Queensberry House)* is incorporated into the Scottish Parliament complex, making it possible for the ghost who is said to live there to look in on the parliamentary sessions for the 129 MPs, held from Tuesday to Thursday. You can also attend the parliamentary meetings. Order your free tickets for the *Public Gallery* in advance as they are in high demand *(tel. 0131 348 5200 or 800 092 7100)*. There are also very interesting 45-minute tours featuring art, politics and architecture. On the photography tour, you will be shown areas of the building that are usually inaccessible.

**INSIDER TIP
Hidden corners**

Book tickets for the tours on days when Parliament is not in session via Eventbrite. If you don't want to join a tour, check out the various 360° videos on the website before visiting. *Mon–Sat 10am–5pm | free admission | Canongate | parliament.scot |* ▯ *h4–5*

🔟 PALACE OF HOLYROODHOUSE 🏁

The Royal Mile becomes really regal at the bottom end. The palace is the king's official residence in Edinburgh. It hasn't always been so beautifully maintained, and was in a poor state of

OLD TOWN

Dramatic cliffs: the view over the city from Salisbury Crags

repair when the young Felix Mendelssohn saw it in 1829: dilapidated, without a roof, and overgrown with ivy. The composer said that this had inspired him to create the somewhat lugubrious oboe melody at the beginning of his romantic *Scottish Symphony*.

Some rooms are open to the public if the monarch is not in town. Holyroodhouse's history is what makes it really fascinating. Its origins lie with King David I. Threatened with being horned by a stag while hunting, he had a vision of the Holy Cross between the animal's antlers and his tragic fate was warded off. After this, the king had the Augustine Order build a monastery to the Holy Cross *(Holy Rood)*. You can walk about the monastery's ruins next to the palace.

A visit to the palace is an absolute must for fans of historical conspiracy theories. This is where Mary Stuart's Italian secretary David Rizzio was murdered in front of the pregnant queen. The Catholic Queen Mary returned from France as a young widow to an austere, Calvinist Edinburgh, where she married her cousin Lord Darnley. He – as well as the Presbyterian clique of the nobility – found his wife's predilection for literature and singing not particularly Scottish. Rizzio, Mary's protégé and possibly her lover, had to be done away with. Darnley himself was assassinated a little later, but that is a different story.

The palace, a fascinating mixture of Scottish baronial style with elements of a French château, ==has a special charm in the early evening, when the setting sun lights up its main façade – Queen Mary would have liked it.== **INSIDER TIP: Sunset glow** The rooms in

36

SIGHTSEEING

the adjacent *Queen's Gallery* show changing exhibitions from the Royal Collection in Windsor Castle. *April–Oct daily 9.30am–6pm, Nov–March daily 9.30am–4.30pm | admission £14 | Canongate | Royal Mile | royalcollection.org.uk |* 🕐 *1 hr |* 📖 *h4*

11 DYNAMIC EARTH

The science museum in a gigantic tent construction below Arthur's Seat is a real hit with children. The journey through time begins with the Big Bang, 14 billion years ago. There's also an earthquake simulator, a volcano eruption installation, a virtual trip through the world of glaciers and the centre of the Earth – all explained with a fresh, lively commentary. Global climatic scenarios can be investigated in the "Future" section. The affiliated *Earthscape Scotland Gallery* explains the geology of the country. There's a fine example outside – the gallery is next to the volcanic peak, Arthur's Seat. The geology lesson is also intended to be a homage to the Edinburgh resident James Hutton (1726–97), who is considered the founder of geological science. *Nov–March Thu–Mon 9.30am–4.30pm, April–Oct Mon–Thu 9.30am–6pm, July–Sept daily | admission £19.50, children £10.50, cheaper to book online | 4 Holyrood Road | dynamicearth.co.uk |* 🕐 *2 hrs |* 📖 *h5*

12 ARTHUR'S SEAT ★

Feel like you're in the Highlands while still in the city. On a clear day, you can see for more than 100km from the top of the most dramatic of the city's three volcanic hills, which has a height of 251m. The remains of the 300-million-year-old volcano from the carboniferous era rise like a rampart to the south of Holyroodhouse in the middle of Holyrood Park. A steep path leads you along the rugged Salisbury Crags to the top, which appeared later as a single dolerite (a rock that was once molten volcanic magma). After just 100m, you will have the finest view of the Parliament Building, and it is only from this perspective that you will be able to fully appreciate how it was slotted into the old city.

If you intend to do the 8km loop to the top, you should be sure to wear sturdy shoes and weatherproof clothing. You might be caught out by the quickly changing weather and the rough terrain. You'll also discover three lakes at the foot of the peaks, as well as solid stone, green meadows, and the dramatic ruins of *St Anthony's Chapel*.

In the park around Arthur's Seat, *Queen's Drive* provides a challenging running spot, and keen cyclists can ride a famous mountain loop, including the 517m-long Innocent Railway Tunnel in the south of the park at the intersection of Newington and St Leonard's streets. The signposted National Cycle Route 1 goes past *Duddingston Loch*, the *Shepp Heid Inn* and *Dr Neil's Garden*. The beginning of the tunnel is just 500m east of the Macau Kitchen restaurant (see p. 62) and a good 5km from *Portobello Beach* (see p. 49). 📖 *J–K6*

INSIDER TIP Cycle trail

OLD TOWN

🔢 SURGEONS' HALL MUSEUMS ⭐

Liver, lungs, lymph – how are the organs, skeleton and nervous system all interconnected? This fantastic museum gets right under the skin, to the places you normally can't see without X-rays. The temple of anatomy was a dissection theatre for surgeons and pathologists from 1832. Everything behind the columned entrance was revamped several years ago and the old operating theatre was even furnished with a digital 3D cadaver – you can explore every corner of the body with a swipe of your hand. Interactivity is complemented by astonishing exhibits and ironic creepiness, such as when you come upon a notebook said to be made of the skin of the grave robber William Burke. You can also find out how doctor and author Arthur Conan Doyle studied here, applying what he learned about anatomy, fingerprinting and forensics to his writing. *Daily 10am–5pm | admission £9 | Nicolson Street | museum.rcsed.ac.uk |* ⏱ *1½ hrs |* 🗺 *g6*

🔢 NATIONAL MUSEUM OF SCOTLAND ⭐

Here, in magnificently grand halls, you can find everything that makes Scotland stand out and what it has gifted to the world. In the atrium, in particular, Victorian royal grandeur is sublimely paired with ultra-modern museum architecture – a dramatic contrast to the spooky, mossy ambiance of the Greyfriars Kirkyard next door. Inside, Scotland presents itself in all its facets: the blade from Edinburgh's guillotine; illuminating information on Dolly the sheep,

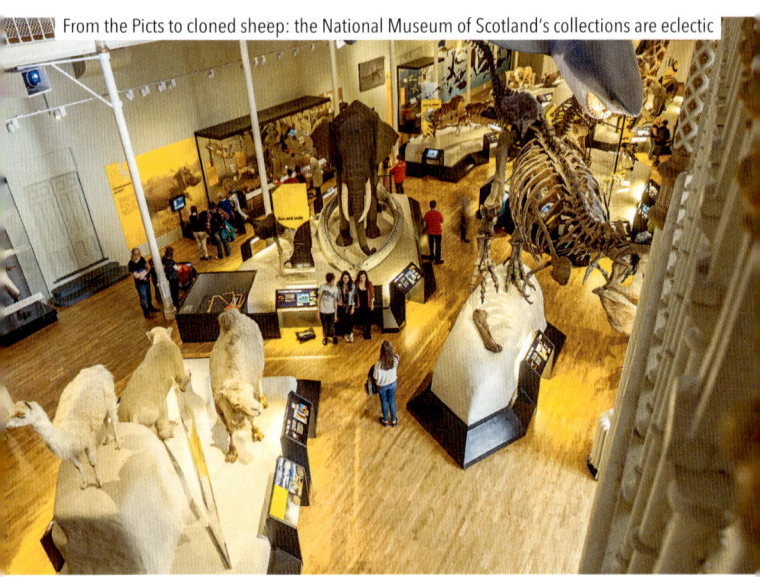

From the Picts to cloned sheep: the National Museum of Scotland's collections are eclectic

SIGHTSEEING

cloned just 10km away in Roslin; stuffed animals and skeletons; and the supposed relics of St Columba, the Irish-Celtic monk who converted the Scottish Picts to Christianity in the sixth century. You'll also find many objects from the world of science and technology, decorative art, design and fashion, including minimalist fashion creations by Jean Muir, who died in 1995 (she had Scottish parents).

> **INSIDER TIP**
> **Hidden histories**
> The *LGBTQIA+ Hidden Histories Trail* explores ten queer highlights from across all the collections.

Among them is the story of renowned mathematician Alan Turing, who cracked the Enigma code during World War II, but was later prosecuted for homosexuality and chemically castrated. A fascinating and truly diverse collection! *Daily 10am–5pm | free admission | Chambers Street/Candlemaker Row | nms.ac.uk | ⏱ 1½–2 hrs | 🚇 f6*

🚩 GREYFRIARS KIRKYARD

It doesn't get more sentimental or touching than this! At the entrance to the churchyard, there's a small monument to a Skye terrier, Greyfriars Bobby, who guarded his master's grave for 14 years after he was buried here. When Bobby himself finally died, he wasn't allowed to join his master in the graveyard (he was a dog, after all). But he has been commemorated since 1872 with this statue.

Greyfriars, the first church built in the city after the Reformation, has a dramatic history. Some 1,200 radical Presbyterians, called Covenanters, who were opposed to the Anglican version of the post-Reformation church imposed by the English king, were forcibly detained here in the middle of the 17th century, and many died.

As well as being the home of Greyfriars Bobby, the churchyard is known for its creepiness and hauntings, and is a regular stop on ghost and horror tours. The stories you will hear will give you goosebumps. Burke and Hare were two 19th-century body snatchers, who dug up corpses to sell to Dr Robert Knox's anatomy school. To satisfy an unceasing demand for cadavers, the two Irishmen became greedy and began to murder to provide them, and were finally discovered when one of the corpses was recognised on the dissection table. The end of the story: Burke was hanged in front of 25,000 people, Hare saved himself by giving evidence against his former partner in crime. Less creepy and more reflective are the classical music concerts in *Greyfriars Kirk* 🐦 *(Thu noon, free admission). April–Oct Mon–Fri 11am–4pm, Sat noon–4pm, Nov–March limited hours | Greyfriars Place | Candlemaker Row/Chambers Street | greyfriarskirk.com | 🚇 f6*

HORROR TOURS 👻

Sooner or later, somebody will thrust a colourful flyer into your hand and entice you into the dark corners of town. Quite a few amateur actors make their living from scaring the wits out of visitors for a couple of hours. A bit like a historical ghost train,

NEW TOWN

professionally performed with costumes and makeup – not for the faint-hearted, but exciting for kids. *Mercat Walking Tours: various themed tours | daily | from £20, children from £15 | tel. 0131 225 5445 | mercattours. com. Witchery Tours (with a lively ghost) | daily | £13, children £9 | tel. 0131 225 6745 | witcherytours.com |* ⏱ *1–2 hrs*

NEW TOWN

Take off your sensible shoes and slip on a smart pair. In the New Town visitors no longer have to find their way along narrow lanes and cobblestones, but can stroll with ease through a genteel, generously proportioned network of streets with uniform three-storey façades, built between 1767 and 1890, with most construction taking place in the Georgian era of the late 18th and early 19th centuries.

Scottish city life plays out on Princes Street

One regularly repeated architectural element is the semicircular fanlight over the front doors on the rows of gracious, typically Georgian town houses (built in the period when all the kings were called George – except for William IV). Sundays are often the best time to wander around and browse the shops in the New Town because there's no work traffic. **INSIDER TIP: Sunday stroll** Even Edinburgh's bankers and office workers come out and relax in the cafés.

Three long, main streets highlight the east–west axis. *George Street*, named after George III, dominates the scene from the ridge of a hill and seems to be the Georgian answer to the medieval Royal Mile. There are many top international – and especially London-based – fashion stores, plus cafés and nightclubs behind the large windows and in the basements. A highlight of a new kind of architectural elegance can be seen on *St Andrew Square* to the east, with the fine department store Harvey Nichols, in *Multrees Walk,* and the new *St James Quarter*. The head of government settled in on the west side of George Street at *Charlotte Square*. The heart of the New Town is bordered by

SIGHTSEEING

NEW TOWN

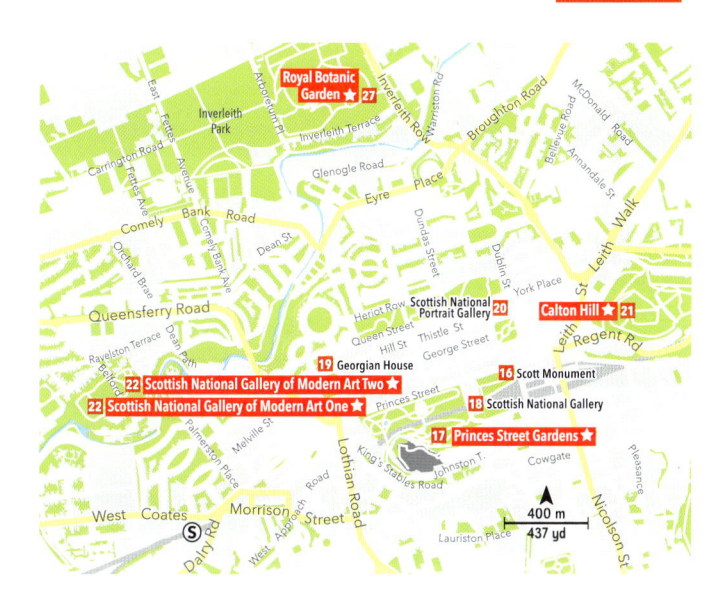

Princes Street and *Queen Street* on either side of George Street. The two, somewhat narrower, *Thistle* and *Rose streets*, named after the national flowers of Scotland and England, with their many inexpensive shops and pubs, are tucked away parallel to the three main streets.

From the north-south streets that cross George Street at regular intervals, you look towards the Old Town on one side, and the Firth of Forth on the other. The wide streets give city cyclists enough space, but George Street is quite steep. The cobblestones fit right in with the Georgian atmosphere, but you'll need good brakes and suspension. The New Town stretches northwards from Queen Street as far as *Fettes College*, Edinburgh's Eton. The circular Georgian residential streets *Royal Circus*, *Moray Place* and *Ainslie Place* are three of the pearls in the crown of the New Town. As in the Old Town, you won't need to use buses: you can see all the sites in a day on foot.

16 SCOTT MONUMENT

The writer's monument to end all writer's monuments is located on Princes Street. After climbing the 287 steps on several levels you will be able to look down on the city. In summer, there are long queues of people at the entrance and the steps get narrower and narrower as you ascend, meaning that some people will only manage the last few at a snail's pace.

NEW TOWN

When Walter Scott died in 1832, the decision was made to create a dramatic monument in his memory. At the time, a neo-Gothic spirit was beginning to emerge in art and architecture, as styles began to change from sober Georgian to ostentatious Victorian. Scott's memorial took the form of an ornate Gothic-style tower made of sandstone, housing 64 figures from the writer's novels and 16 busts of other Scottish poets. Today, the 61m-high construction stands like a church spire without a base. *Daily usually 10am–3.30pm | admission £8 | East Princes Street Gardens | edinburghmuseums.org.uk | f4*

🟥 PRINCES STREET GARDENS ★

The gardens are Edinburgh's green lungs, popular for summer sunbathing and a location for events. The lake where women accused of being witches and rubbish were disposed of was drained around 1800, when the New Town was being built. The resulting park landscape stretches along the south side of the entire length of Princes Street, which was not built up on the park side so as not to obstruct the view of the Old Town skyline. The *East Gardens* are dominated by the Scott Monument and continue to *Waverley Station* – the main railway station named after a series of novels by Walter Scott – and the *Fruit Market Gallery*. By the way, the clock on the tower of the Balmoral Hotel, near the railway station, is four minutes fast to prevent passengers from missing their trains.

> **INSIDER TIP** That clock's fast!

It only shows the correct time on New Year's Eve. A train leaves Waverley every 15 minutes for Glasgow and the charming concourse is also worth taking a look at. From mid-November, there's a well-stocked *Christmas market behind the Scott Monument as well as an ice-skating rink* and more (edinburgh-christmas.com). On the southern end of the station, the *Dungeons* chamber of horrors *(usually Mon–Fri 11am–4pm, Sat, Sun 11am–5pm or 6pm | timeslots booked online approx. £ 18.50, open ticket £28 (usually 18 years and over) | 32 Market Street | thedungeons.com/edinburgh)* is a cavern full of scary figures, something for the intrepid to enjoy.

> **INSIDER TIP** Edinburgh's Christmas

A steep street, *The Mound*, divides the park and leads up to the Old Town; on the way, the temple-like architecture of the *Royal Scottish Academy* and *Scottish National Gallery* may make you slow down a bit as you stride past them with a ceremonial air. In the gallery, there's a relief of the hilly city to look at. The *West Gardens* are a wonderful place for a stroll, a climb up to the castle or for simply enjoying the view. This is also a very popular meeting place for many locals. In summer, the aroma of coffee wafts out of the *Open Air Café*, water bubbles in a fountain, flowers add touches of colour and the fair-skinned Scots attempt to get a bit of a sun tan. The people of Edinburgh love their popular park on the slope and have a great time there. It is the stage for the

SIGHTSEEING

loudest music and festival events in the city, and there's an especially festive atmosphere in the evening, looking across at the castle.

Things become more picturesque and atmospheric at the western end of Princes Street Gardens. This is where St Cuthbert's Churchyard connects with two churches: St Cuthbert's Kirk *(5 Lothian Road | st-cuthberts.net)* is a stately, roundish basilica in the midst of the green of the trees with an interior decorated in warm tones; St John's *(3 Lothian Road | stjohns-edinburgh.org.uk)*, on the other hand, is an overpowering Victorian construction built in the late-Gothic Perpendicular style and decorated with the most exquisite church windows in town. Especially in winter, the gravestones in the cemetery provide a fabulous foreground for photos of the castle when there are no leaves on the trees to block the view. *Princes Street | d–f 4–5*

18 SCOTTISH NATIONAL GALLERY

The National Gallery is enveloped in an aura of Greek antiquity, mainly due to the neoclassical columned façade of the two main buildings, designed by New Town architect William Playfair. You don't even have to go inside – just enjoy the atmosphere created by the self-appointed orators and chattering little groups outside. Eventually the incessant sound of bagpipes may force you inside. Here, you can enjoy countless paintings by old masters, impressionists and expressionists, and important Scottish painters, all hung closely together. The *Royal Scottish Academy Building (royalscottishacademy.org)*, where you will be

Princes Street Gardens are Edinburgh's Central Park

43

NEW TOWN

asked to pay for special exhibitions, also belongs to the National Gallery.

A third modern wing connects the 19th-century temples and offers sanctuary in its café. A certain kind of cult has developed around the portrait of *The Reverend Robert Walker Skating on Duddingston Loch*, painted by Henry Raeburn in 1795. It shows the vicar of Canongate Church wearing a frock coat and top hat skating on one leg, which was a requirement for joining the *Edinburgh Skating Society*. A dozen delicate watercolours by William Turner are displayed every January, when the winter light can do them the least damage – this was stipulated by the people who donated the artwork. *Daily 10am–5pm | free admission | 72 The Mound | nationalgalleries.org | 1–2 hrs | e5*

INSIDER TIP: Turners in January

GEORGIAN HOUSE
Here, in the green of Charlotte Square, you can take a peek into the parlours of Georgian upper-middle class of Edinburgh, where intellectuals, like the inventor of the telephone Alexander Graham Bell, founder of hospital hygiene Joseph Lister, and Field Marshal Douglas Haig, lived. Today, the square is the home of the head of the government, at no. 6.

From the outside, house no. 7 is a typical terraced house at the northern end of Charlotte Square with a neo-classical, symmetrical façade in the style of architect Robert Adams. The uniformity of the layout continues on the inside, where it also contrasts with the cosy furnishings. The lack of carpets in the Georgian era contrasts with the later, more lavish Victorian period. The kitchen and dining room are real eye-catchers and you may well feel like sitting down at the opulent table. The charming National Trust stewards know how to stop that, but they will let you in on the most intimate secrets of high society between 1714 and 1837. *Daily March–Oct 10am–5pm, Nov Wed–Sun 10am–4pm | admission £12 | 7 Charlotte Square | nts.org.uk | 45 mins | D4*

SCOTTISH NATIONAL PORTRAIT GALLERY
This is where you can find the *Who's Who* of Scottish society captured in every kind of portrait imaginable: an exhibition of Scottish heroes from Sean Connery, Irvine Welsh and Alex Ferguson to Bonnie Prince Charlie and – of course – Mary Stuart. Paintings are complemented by an outstanding collection of photography. The entrance hall itself is a real eye-catcher. *Daily 10am–5pm | free admission | 1 Queen Street | nationalgalleries.org | 1 hr | F4*

CALTON HILL ★
Nowhere else offers a more romantic end to the day and, shortly before sunset, photographers haul their tripods up the volcanic hill. Fill your rucksack with bread, cheese and wine and head uphill to savour the experience. As the sun disappears, the Balmoral Hotel and the castle are illuminated focal points,

INSIDER TIP: Sunset picnic & panorama

44

SIGHTSEEING

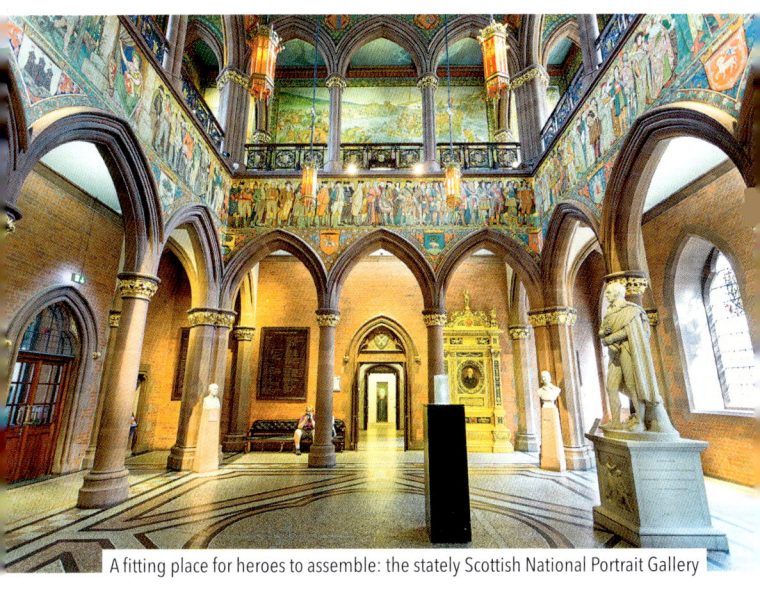

A fitting place for heroes to assemble: the stately Scottish National Portrait Gallery

and the traffic on *Princes Street* runs in a line of light towards the west. The silhouette of the Old Town, with *Arthur's Seat* and the castle, dominates the view to the left and, to the right, the eye swings towards the rooftop of *St James Quarter* and the *Firth of Forth*.

There is a strange collection of monuments on the hill, which give the impression of having been placed here due to lack of space elsewhere. The 12 Doric columns designed by Edinburgh's neoclassical builder William Henry Playfair were erected in 1822 as a *National Monument*. Inspired by a Greek temple, it was planned as a bombastic war memorial, but the funding ran out. Today it's ruined, but it still has people gazing up at it on the eastern horizon from Princes Street.

Next to it, the 32m-high tower (143 steps) of the *Nelson Monument (closed at the time of publication)* honours the victors in the Battle of Trafalgar with an even more exposed view. At the top of the tower, which looks like a telescope, there's a large time ball, which has been dropped every day since 1853 to tell sailors in the Leith port and Firth of Forth that it is 1pm. Alongside this visual time signal, the one o'clock gun was introduced in 1861 on the castle's hill. Today, the ball still falls when the cannon shot goes off.

The monumental duo of the tower and columns is complemented by Playfair's temple-like *City Observatory*, a small memorial temple – another Greek inspiration – for the Edinburgh moral philosopher Dugald Stewart (1753–1828) and a monument to

OTHER SIGHTS

From city to village: exploring Stockbridge

local mathematician John Playfair (1748–1819).

The neoclassical romanticism of the hilltop was joined by modern features in 2018. The observatory and nearby City Dome house modern art with temporary exhibitions, complemented by the new gallery *Hill Side (Thu–Sun 10am–5pm)*. The northwestern side of the complex is home to the fine restaurant *The Lookout* – a small glass building on a cantilever. Drink a toast to the city from your table, protected from the weather. The food is created by the same people as in the *Gardener's Cottage* at the foot of Calton Hill. *collective-edinburgh.art | ewh.org.uk | G3–4*

OTHER SIGHTS

Edinburgh exudes rural charm in Dean Village and Stockbridge, to the west of the city centre, and the Water of Leith is a great place for a stroll and a cycle.

The small river known as the Water of Leith creates a natural border between the elegant façades of the residential roads of the New Town and the hidden houses and suburban streets of shops of Stockbridge. It's worth taking a stroll along *Raeburn Place* here. Visit the city's most pleasant market

INSIDER TIP
Sunday market

SIGHTSEEING

🐟 *Modern One (📖 A5)* – from Matisse to Hockney and Pollock, alongside representatives of various modern Scottish art movements. Charles Jencks' landscape sculpture sits in front of the entrance. The café provides great refreshments.

The 🐟 *Scottish National Gallery of Modern Art Two (📖 B4)*, opposite, is more intimate. The exhibitions are dominated by Surrealism and Dadaism, and there's also a replica of the studio where Eduardo Paolozzi (1924–2005), Edinburgh's greatest modern artist, once worked. There's a nice café here, too. *Daily 10am–5pm | free admission | 75 Belford Road | nationalgalleries.org | Bus 13*

23 LEITH ★

Leith has become cool. Some 3km north of the city, the old port area was once stuck in the past, but the cobbled enclave around *Bernhard Street Bridge* near the mouth of the Water of Leith has blossomed into a charming hub. It's now a very popular place for going out, lined with cosy cafés, pubs, and eateries – including Michelin-starred restaurants (see p. 58 and p. 60) – especially since the new tram line opened in 2023, making the journey so much quicker. The main street, *Leith Walk*, has rebounded from the bad reputation it gained when it featured in the film version of *Trainspotting* back in the 1990s.

The 2km journey from the city to the Foot of the (Leith) Walk has a rugged charm, adorned with cool local shops and cafés popular with young locals. The tram then travels through the

---

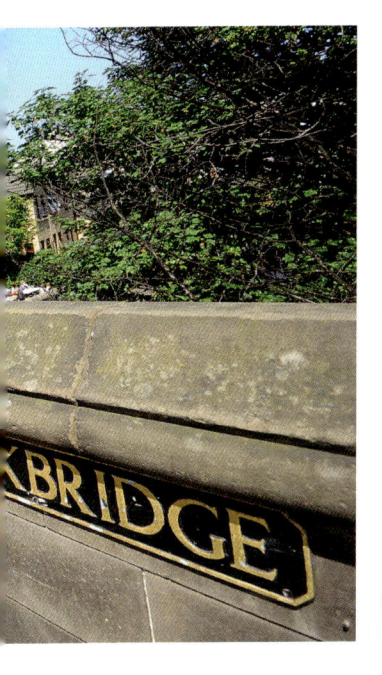

==on the bridge over the river *(Sun 10am–4pm | Saunders/Kerr Street)* – and have some delicious paella!==

The quiet, idyllic paths along the river take you to the picturesque Dean Village and to temples of modern art. In the opposite direction, you can walk or cycle as far as *Leith*, where the port has developed into a place for gourmets and night owls. *Portobello Beach* is 5km south of here.

22 SCOTTISH NATIONAL GALLERY OF MODERN ART ★

A rich collection: two temples of modern art next to each other. The best art museum in town is located on the edge of Dean Village. The international artistic universe of the past hundred years is represented here in

OTHER SIGHTS

Shore restaurant mile on to the somewhat forgotten *Ocean Terminal* shopping centre, with the *Royal Yacht Britannia*, a new whisky distillery and on to the small-scale fishing port of *Newhaven*, which has some great fish and chip shops. To the west lie Cramond Isle, beaches and the Forth Bridge. 📖 *K–M 1–2*

24 PORT OF LEITH DISTILLERY
Two local whisky lovers have fulfilled their dream in this tower, a unique location for a distillery.

INSIDER TIP
Gin before whisky

They also produce *Lind & Lime Gin* in an attractive bottle (a great souvenir!) as a reminder of the glass that used to be made here. It's tiding them over until their first Scotch is distilled. *Next to the Royal Yacht Britannia | leithdistillery.com |* 📖 *L1*

25 ROYAL YACHT BRITANNIA ★ 🐾
Queen Elizabeth II used this cruise ship (it's not a yacht in the usual sense of the word) from 1953 until it was decommissioned in 1997. It's said she loved her time on *Britannia*, but the ship also served a purpose for the state, because it allowed her to play host to official guests while abroad. The style is pretty typical of the taste of post-war Britain, with some Art Deco features. The audio-guide is useful to understand what you're seeing. Visitors board the queen-sized yacht in the port of Leith through the *Ocean Terminal* (with its own shopping centre), planned by star designer Terence Conran. *Nov–March 10am–5pm, April–Aug 9.30am–6pm, Sept 10am–6pm, Oct 10am–5.30pm | admission £18.25 | Ocean Drive, Leith | royalyachtbritannia.co.uk | Tram Ocean Terminal, bus 200 Skylink/Ocean Drive |* 📖 *K1*

26 CRAMOND ISLE
A walk on the wild side! A spot of wilderness, one mile offshore in the Firth of Forth, beckons you to take a gamble with the tides. The little island is halfway between Leith and the Forth Bridges, and it's accessed from the mainland by a causeway. It's best to only make the journey two hours either side of low tide, otherwise you'll be stuck there for six hours. It's a great 7km cycle ride from *Newhaven Harbour*. There's a fish sculpture on the beach just before the causeway. Afterwards, toast your trip out to sea with a pint in the rustic *Cramond Inn (£). Bus 41 |* 📖 *I1*

27 ROYAL BOTANIC GARDEN ★ 🐾
Here, Scotland is in full bloom. The gardens are famous for their floral splendour, along with the great landscaped gardens of Scotland's west coast. Dating from 1670, the garden has long been an important place for research. With its rock and Chinese gardens, and (ten) wonderful glasshouses, it's the only subtropical location you'll find in Edinburgh! It also has the oldest collections of botanical literature in Great Britain.

The view of the city's medieval skyline from the *Terrace Café (March–Sept*

SIGHTSEEING

The Royal Botanic Garden combines rugged Scotland and delicate floral displays

daily 10am-5.30pm | tel. 0131 552 0616 | £) is a real delight. *Daily, Oct, Feb 10am-5pm, Nov-Jan 10am-4pm, March-Sept 10am-6pm | glasshouses closed for renovation at time of publication |* 🐷 *admission free | Arboretum Place, Stockbridge | rbge.org.uk | bus 23, 27 (from The Mound/Princes Street) |* ⏱ *1½-3 hrs |* 📖 *C-D 1-2*

28 EDINBURGH ZOO

It's a good idea to get the shuttle to start at the top of this hilly zoo. Then wander down the hill past the koalas, rhinoceroses and other animals. Children love the penguin parade *(April-Aug 2.15pm, check online)*. Don't set off without a packed lunch! Pre-booked time slots are available online. *April-Sept daily 10am-6pm, Oct, March daily 10am-5pm, Nov-Feb daily 10am-4pm | admission £24.25, children over 3 £15.25 | 134 Corstorphine Road, Murrayfield | edinburghzoo.org.uk | bus 12, 26, 31, 900 Zoo |* 📖 *l1*

29 PORTOBELLO

Its claim to be the "Brighton of the North" may be a bit of an exaggeration, but the long, sandy beach only about 30 minutes by bus from Princes Street is a very cool spot on hot summer days. Enjoy the long promenade, the typical, nostalgic Victorian seaside charm, the cafés, pubs, ice cream and chips, and the unusual-looking houses on the streets behind the beach. *Bus 21, 26, 49 |* 📖 *m1*

DAY TRIPS

🔟 DEEP SEA WORLD

20km from Edinburgh / 30 mins by train

Dive into an underwater world. First, take the train over the famous red Forth Rail Bridge to North Queensferry on the Firth of Forth. Travelators take visitors along tunnels through an aquarium with sharks, rays, schools of fish and seals. With a supervised diving session for beginners, you can swim among sand sharks and rays in their own environment (from £140). Watch the seahorses and sharks get fed daily at 2.30pm; online booking 48 hours in advance means you save up to 20 per cent. *Daily 10am–5pm, shorter opening hours in winter | admission £17, 3–12s £12.25 | Forthside Terrace, North Queensferry | deepseaworld.com | Fife Circle Line from Waverley to North Queensferry | /1*

3️⃣1️⃣ GLASGOW

75km from Edinburgh / 50 mins by train

Scotland's largest city, with a population of around 750,000, is only a 50-minute train ride away from Edinburgh's Waverley Station. There are several departures every hour. Glasgow is very different to Edinburgh: it's a vibrant city centre, with some post-industrial urban landscapes, a strong dialect and a lively culture. Glasgow is more diverse, more hectic and less relaxed than Edinburgh. Its no-frills charm, including in the parts that are somewhat frayed at the edges, like the East End, appeals to many

Often dull and *dreich*, life in Glasgow is more appealing than the weather

SIGHTSEEING

visitors. Unlike the more refined residents of Edinburgh, Glaswegians tend not to mince their words.

As soon as you leave *Queen Street Station*, you will feel the big-city atmosphere. As a global centre for shipbuilding and home to rich merchants 150 years ago, Glasgow displayed its wealth and Victorian confidence in lavish official buildings. Carrara marble was used to build the Renaissance *City Chambers* around 1890. Next to it, the renovated post-industrial *Merchant City* pulsates with life. The old stores are now full of boutiques, art galleries, bars, restaurants and a market. Fans of Art Nouveau will find a comprehensive collection of work by Charles Rennie Mackintosh at the *Lighthouse* architecture museum.

The underground and bus offer good access to the green West End of the city, with its university, and the Scots' favourite museum, the *Kelvingrove Art Gallery (glasgowlife.org.uk)*, in the park of the same name. At the end of your day out, you should definitely visit the River Clyde, once a centre for shipbuilding. Now, the *Riverside Museum (glasgowlife.org.uk/museums)*, to the south of Kelvingrove, explains the exciting history of transport in a building designed by star architect Zara Hadid. Up the river to the east, there are some new landmarks, such as the *Glasgow Science Centre (glasgowsciencecentre.org)*, with its high tower.

To enjoy dinner with an international flavour, leave the Clyde and head to the *Finniestown* district. Walk or cycle to the iconic *Scotia Bar (112 Stockwell Street)* for beer, live folk music and interesting people, just over a kilometre south of Queen Street station. A city bike is ideal for exploring the area around the Clyde. You can hire them near the Riverside Museum *(nextbike.co.uk). peoplemakeglasgow.com* | m k1–2

32 ROSSLYN CHAPEL

12km from Edinburgh, 50 mins by bus from Princes Street

This fascinating, mysterious chapel became well known thanks to Dan Brown's novel *The Da Vinci Code*. It is situated about 12km south of Edinburgh in the village of Roslin (where Dolly, the cloned sheep, was born). A visitor centre provides explanations for the enigmatic stone carvings that cover almost every inch of the chapel. Some are Christian in nature but the most famous feature the Green Man – a traditional pagan figure representing fertility. No photography is allowed inside. *Daily 9am–5pm, eight bookable timeslots lasting 90 mins each | admission £9.50 | Chapel Loan | rosslynchapel.com | bus 37 Roslin Hotel |* 1 hr | m m1

EATING & DRINKING

Edinburgh's restaurants are booming! The Scots have always placed great value on their Angus beef, as well as the fish, scallops and oysters from the rivers and the sea. In recent years, a new creativity – often with roots in France, the Mediterranean and Asia – has found its way into their preparation.

Simple food, such as fish and chips and lasagne, has become much tastier, while in gastropubs menus are just as important as the list of whiskies and ales. Restaurants and gastropubs focus on local produce, such as pheasant and mussels, and menus usually feature

> You'll find all the venues in this chapter on the pull-out map

A Scottish maritime hit: smoked fish soup called cullen skink

vegetarian and vegan options. Traditional dishes, such as black pudding and haggis have not been forgotten – but today they are creatively refined. Asian restaurants enrich the culinary scene, and some pubs also serve curries.

The once-depressed port of Leith has blossomed into a culinary centre with Michelin-starred restaurants – but without being flashy. Food is often served from noon to 2pm and from 6pm to 10pm, but some places are open all day, and the city's cafés are great for quelling your hunger before dinner time.

WHERE EDINBURGH EATS

MARCO POLO HIGHLIGHTS

★ **VALVONA & CROLLA**
Italian sensuality contrasts with the sober lines of the New Town ➤ p. 56

★ **URBAN ANGEL**
Edinburgh's most popular café-brasserie relies on organic and Fairtrade ingredients ➤ p. 57

★ **DAVID BANN**
Top-quality, creative vegetarian cuisine in the Old Town ➤ p. 60

★ **MACAU KITCHEN**
Take a trip to the Far East: a wonderful blending of Portuguese and Chinese flavours ➤ p. 62

OLD TOWN
Vaulted ceilings, candlelight, Baroque splendour: creative cuisine meets the Middle Ages

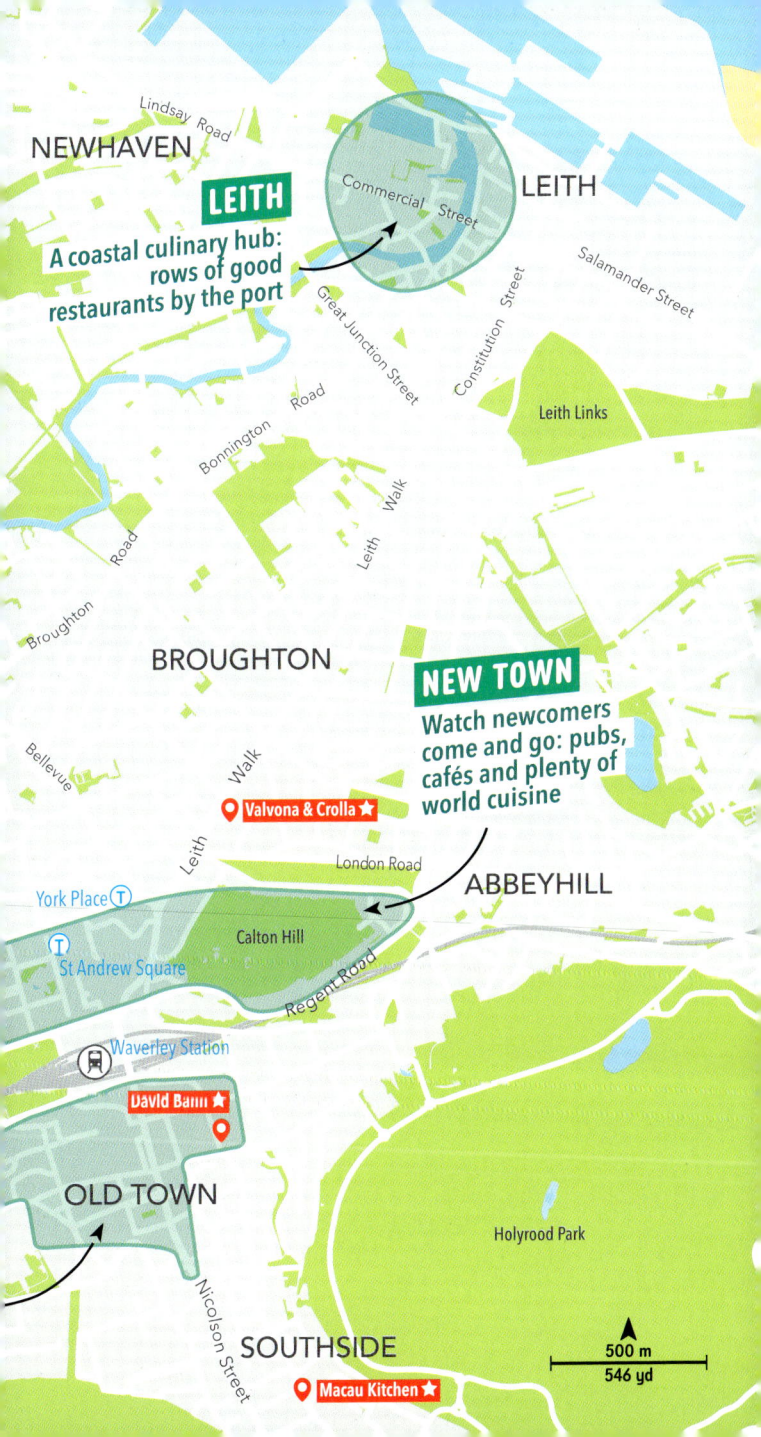

LEITH
A coastal culinary hub: rows of good restaurants by the port

NEW TOWN
Watch newcomers come and go: pubs, cafés and plenty of world cuisine

NEWHAVEN — Lindsay Road

LEITH — Commercial Street, Great Junction Street, Constitution Street, Salamander Street, Leith Links

BROUGHTON — Bonnington Road, Broughton Road, Bellevue, Leith Walk

NEW TOWN / ABBEYHILL — London Road, Calton Hill, Regent Road, York Place, St Andrew Square

- Valvona & Crolla ★
- David Bann ★
- Macau Kitchen ★

Waverley Station

OLD TOWN

SOUTHSIDE — Nicolson Street

Holyrood Park

500 m / 546 yd

CAFÉS & CAFÉ/RESTAURANTS

CAFÉS & CAFÉ/RESTAURANTS

1 COLONNADES@THE SIGNET LIBRARY

The most elegant tearoom in Edinburgh, set in a spacious Georgian library hall. It has a fantastic New Town feel, but is actually in the Old Town. Fancy a hearty soup for lunch? Even better, book in advance and dive into the full-blown afternoon tea *(11am–4.30pm, £60)*. A heritage atmosphere at its best. *Closed Sat | Parliament Square | Old Town | tel. 0131 226 1064 | thesignetlibrary.co.uk | f5*

2 TOAST

A great café for breakfast and brunch on the banks of Leith. You can also dine here in the evening from Thursday to Saturaday, enjoying organic wine with your meal. Popular brunch dishes include American pancakes, shakshuka and avocado on sourdough bread. The (gluten-free) cakes are very good: the éclairs are particularly tasty. *Daily | 65 The Shore | Leith | tel. 0131 467 6984 | toastleith.co.uk | L2*

3 THE HAVEN CAFÉ

The Haven sits inconspicuously between Leith and Newhaven, and serves divine, homemade (late) breakfasts, such as a haggis, cheese and chilli jam sourdough toastie. The pistachio and berry cake is equally delicious, the pancakes are great and the coffee is sublime. *Daily until 4pm | 9 Anchorfield | Newhaven | tel. 0131 467 7513 | FB | I1*

4 VALVONA & CROLLA ★

This Italian delicatessen and café, with hams hanging from the ceiling and the aroma of coffee, cheese, pastries and freshly baked bread in the air, is the result of a wave of Italian emigration to Scotland more than 100 years ago. Enter the magical world of delicious breakfast and first-rate lunch creations in Broughton. *Daily | 19 Elm Row | Broughton | tel. 0131 556 6066 | valvonacrolla.co.uk | G3*

5 MASONS BAKERY

A neighbourhood bakery without the frills. The pies are the best. Why come here? Because you can sit opposite on the port wall with mermaid graffiti and eat your pie with a view of the fishing boats. *Tue–Sat until 2pm | 1 Starbank Road | Newhaven | I1*

INSIDER TIP Pie by the bay

6 HERBIE

A takeaway café amid the hustle and bustle of the West End, with a table at the front. It seems like every fourth passerby goes in and comes out with fresh sandwiches, or a tasty soup in a paper cup with home-baked bread. Sit down, enjoy your soup and watch the world go by. Then walk on to Dean Village. *Mon–Fri until 5pm | 7 William Street | West End | C5*

7 THE MILKMAN

Such an Old Town feel – complete with a famous old façade! Lean against the stone walls or sit inside, or on Cockburn Street, and enjoy the buzzing atmosphere. After your sublime

EATING & DRINKING

coffee, treat yourself to something at *Juwelier Perre (no. 5)* or record shop *Underground Solu'shn (no. 9). Daily until 5pm | 7 Cockburn Street | Old Town | Instagram: themilkmancoffee | ⊞ f5*

GASTROPUBS & BISTROS

8 BREWHEMIA

A statement, bold Scottish beer hall took over what had been a dilapidated sports bar. The result: delicious pimped-up porridge and sourdough flatbreads in the morning; beer, prosecco and burgers right up to midnight, with live bands and large tables – in short, an all-day event. *Daily | 1a Market Street | Old Town | tel. 0131 226 9560 | brewhemia.co.uk | ⊞ f5*

9 CITY CAFÉ

A true American-style diner with relatively low prices for burgers and drinks. 🐖 Breakfast is available until the evening (9am to 10pm) to suit night owls, and happy hour is from 5pm to 8pm. *Daily | 19 Blair Street | Old Town | tel. 0131 220 0125 | the citycafe.co.uk | ⊞ f5*

10 URBAN ANGEL ★

Wooden tables and natural stone floors are matched by free-range, seasonal ingredients in this popular café. Breakfast is served from 9am, and locals flock here for lunch and weekend brunch. The products are local; the fish, game and mozzarella are Scottish, often organic and fairly traded. *Mon–Fri 9am–3.30pm,*

INSIDER TIP
The best brunch

The scent (and the look) of Italy: Mediterranean dreams in Valvona & Crolla

RESTAURANTS £££

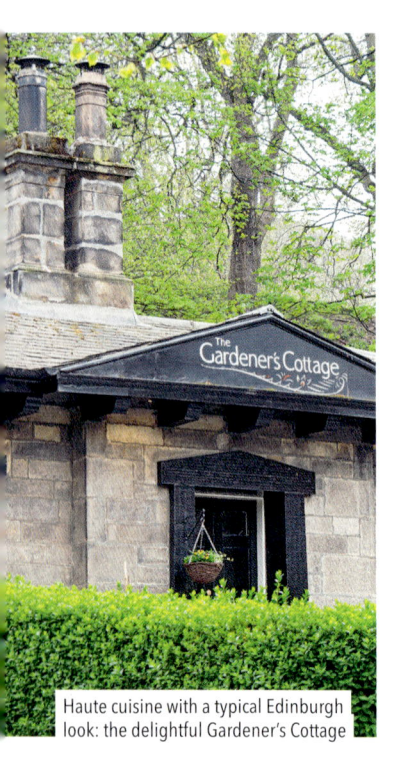

Haute cuisine with a typical Edinburgh look: the delightful Gardener's Cottage

Sat/Sun until 4.30pm | 121 Hanover Street | New Town | tel. 0131 225 6215 | urban-angel.co.uk | E4

11 KING'S WARK

In the 17th century, this was a residence, storehouse and armoury for King James I. Its wood floors and panelling, and rustic exposed stone, are still reminiscent of days gone by. Since the revival of Leith, this well-known, popular pub has been spruced up. The generous servings of sophisticated pub grub, however, remain. *Daily | 36 The Shore | Leith | tel. 0131 554 9260 | kingswark.co.uk | bus 12, 16, 22 | L2*

RESTAURANTS £££

12 TIMBERYARD

This top restaurant, housed in a 19th-century warehouse and run by the Radford family, has a historical feel, and a modern, creative and sustainable menu, with dishes made using regional British ingredients. It got its first Michelin star in 2023, making the Timberyard the first Edinburgh restaurant to receive this acknowledgement outside Leith. The five-course menu is £99; the tasting menu is £129. *Thu 4-11pm, Fri-Sun noon-11pm | 10 Lady Lawson Street | Old Town | tel. 0131 221 1222 | timberyard.co | d6*

13 HERON

Named after the well-known water bird, this magnificent pub on the Leith has had a Michelin star since 2023. The young chefs are particularly focused on producing modern food with traditional Scottish ingredients, and the vegetarian tasting menu is as enjoyable as a stroll through the gardens and woods. *Sat, Sun lunch, Wed-Sun dinner | 87-91A Henderson Street | Leith | tel. 0131 554 1242 | heron.scot | L2*

14 THE GARDENER'S COTTAGE & LOOKOUT BY GARDENER'S COTTAGE

Top-quality sister restaurants: the *Cottage* at the foot of Calton Hill and the *Lookout* at the top. Here, you will enjoy very creative Scottish cuisine in a building with wraparound windows, and a famous view. In the *Cottage*, the atmosphere is more intimate, with

EATING & DRINKING

Today's recommendations

Breakfast

KIPPERS
Salted, smoked herrings, often cooked in milk

PORRIDGE
Porridge oats with milk

FULL SCOTTISH
Potato scone, baked beans, egg, bacon, mushrooms, sausages

Lunch

COCK-A-LEEKIE
Chicken soup with leek, often thickened with rice or barley. Prunes are sometimes added

CULLEN SKINK
Smoked-fish soup with milk, potatoes and onions

OYSTERS
Mainly from Scotland's west or north coast

SCALLOPS
Usually from the Orkney Islands

SKIRLIE
Oatmeal groats served with onions

Mains

HAGGIS
Sheep's stomach stuffed with sheep offal and oatmeal

BLACK PUDDING
Blood and oat sausage

ROAST GROUSE

STOVIES
Stewed beef with onions (usually made from leftovers)

POACHED SMOKED HADDOCK
Often served with poached eggs

Desserts & tea

CRANACHAN
Whipped cream with toasted oatmeal, honey, whisky and berries

ARRAN BLUE
Soft blue cheese from the Isle of Arran

SCONES WITH CLOTTED CREAM

RESTAURANTS ££

long tables and a daily-changing seasonal menu from the sea and garden. The *Cottage* opening times depend on the time of year, see the website. Cottage: *1 London Road | New Town | tel. 0131 677 0244 | thegardeners cottage.co | G3*; Lookout: *Wed–Sat | Calton Hill | New Town | tel. 0131 322 1246 | thelookoutedinburgh.co | bus 1, 4, 19 Leopold Place | G4*

15 THE WITCHERY BY THE CASTLE

Dine in opulence in a unique 16th-century atmosphere. When you enter the dark, moody and sumptuously decorated space, you will be able to imagine the ghosts of drowned witches roaming around. The restaurant serves sophisticated Scottish cuisine and is linked to the brighter and more modern *Secret Garden*. 🐷 The two-course lunch is interesting and costs £34.50. *Daily | Castlehill | Old Town | tel. 0131 225 5613 | thewitchery.com | e5*

16 RESTAURANT MARTIN WISHART

Martin Wishart is known as one of the half dozen star chefs in Edinburgh, and is responsible for other kitchens in the city and across the country. He was the first chef to receive a Michelin star in his home country, in 2001. He cooks French cuisine with fresh ingredients from the water and land of Scotland in Leith. His restaurant is modestly tucked away between affordable café-restaurants. Inside, the atmosphere is quiet, with warm wood panelling. The likes of snail ravioli and Orkney scallops may be served as part of a tasting menu, but they may also appear on the 🐷 affordable three-course lunch (menu £60). *Closed Sun–Thu | 54 The Shore | Leith | tel. 0131 553 3557 | restaurantmartin wishart.co.uk | bus 22 to The Shore | L2*

17 THE KITCHIN

The industrial grey tones and natural stone of the interior of Tom Kitchin's extraordinary gourmet address create a feeling for the past history of this former whisky toll house. The Edinburgh chef has had his Michelin star for over 15 years; he serves all that Scotland has to offer coupled with French refinement. Sea urchins, rabbit or beef – this is how straightforwardly the dishes are listed on the menu. Tasting menus from £140. *Closed Sun, Mon | 78 Commercial Quay | Leith | tel. 0131 555 1755 | thekitchin.com | tram: Port of Leith, bus 16, 35 Sandport Street | L1*

RESTAURANTS ££

18 DAVID BANN ★

It is hard to imagine Scottish cooking without meat, and this is what makes this excellent vegetarian restaurant in the Old Town so special. The risottos, *galettes*, polentas and homemade ravioli are all delicious and can even convince meat-eaters to sample vegetarian fare. Vegans will also find good dishes here. You should try the *kelpie ale* brewed from seaweed. *Daily | 56–58 St Mary's Street | Old Town | tel. 0131 556 5888 | davidbann.com | g5*

INSIDER TIP Beer made with seaweed

EATING & DRINKING

The Kitchin: incredible food and chic minimalist industrial design

19 HOTEL DU VIN BISTRO

Although this hotel restaurant belongs to an exclusive chain of hotels, it has its own distinctive look, with a setting reminiscent of a castle cellar. The stylish conversion of the inner courtyard of a former hospital is a rare thing to find, even in Edinburgh. The kitchen combines Scottish and French cuisine, serving dishes such as steak and snail pie. The petits fours with berry marshmallows and the Turkish delight flavoured with Irn-Bru, Scotland's national soft drink, are fun. You can enjoy a rainy afternoon by having afternoon tea here, with tasty canapés and ceremonial tea. *Daily | 11 Bristol Place | Old Town | tel. 0131 247 4900 | hotelduvin.com | f6*

20 THE LITTLE CHART ROOM

A warm-hearted, modish neighbourhood bistro with muted colours and dark-wood floors. The focus is on a creative modern approach to local ingredients, with touches of Asia thrown in, such as in a main of cod, BBQ maitake mushrooms, peas, lollo blonde, brown shrimp, nori and elderflower butter. Set menus and wine pairings are available. *Mon–Thu 6–8pm, Fri/Sat 1–2pm, 6–8.30pm, Sun 1–2pm, 6–8pm | 14 Bonnington Road | Bonnington | tel. 0131 556 6600 | thelittlechartroom.com | L2*

21 HAKATAYA

Small Japanese restaurant in an alleyway in the New Town, serving authentic dishes like *tonkotsu ramen* from Fukuoka and typical dishes from Japanese *izakaya* pubs. Ramen features too, of course, alongside homemade sushi. *Daily lunch, dinner | 120/122 Rose Street | New Town | tel. 0131 629 3320 | hakatayauk.com | d5*

RESTAURANTS £

Great for people-watching through the large front window: The Olive Branch

KALPNA
Not just any Indian – this is the Gujarati/Punjabi restaurant that has been on everyone's lips for over 25 years, serving the best vegetarian and vegan cuisine. The all-you-can-eat lunchtime buffet is always popular. *Daily | 2–3 St Patrick Square | New Town | tel. 0131 667 9890 | kalpnarestaurant.com | G6*

INSIDER TIP: Indian buffet

MACAU KITCHEN ★
Enchanting Macanese-Portuguese cuisine, 20 minutes south of the Royal Mile. The well-travelled owners cook, and aromas from around the globe mix with the warm, friendly atmosphere. What a blend: hearty Portuguese tastes melding with aromatic Asian flavours. The place isn't very big, but it is popular, so make sure you reserve. It's not licensed but you can bring your own drink. A culinary journey in the marvellous Holyrood Park. *Closed Mon, Tue | 93 St Leonard's Street | Newington | tel. 757 766 7334 | bus 14 Parkside Street | G7*

RESTAURANTS £

THE ALEXANDER GRAHAM BELL
Affordable fun on George Street. Thanks to the Wetherspoons pub chain, this expensive road offers a great deal on fish and chips with a pint, and other meal combinations. The pub interior is rather fine – the walls are adorned with large portraits of Scottish geniuses, including Bell, the first person to bring the telephone to market. *Daily | 62–66 George Street | New Town | tel. 0131 240 8220 | jdwetherspoon.com | D4*

THE OLIVE BRANCH
See and be seen: this café-restaurant, with its post-industrial design, is the most popular in the fashionable Broughton district. You can sit by the large windows and take in the fascinating mix of customers and what's going on outside on the street. The servings of roast and fried food are generous. Popular place for Sunday brunch from 10am. *Closed Mon |*

EATING & DRINKING

91 Broughton Street | New Town | tel. 0131 557 8589 | theolivebranch scotland.co.uk | F3

26 BABA

Levantine cuisine has made a move into New Town thanks to Baba. Meals composed of its many tasty meze dishes are the flavour of the month. Mains veer away from the traditional Lebanese meat grills to include fish (with harissa) and steak (with sumac-infused onions). *Daily | 130 George Street | New Town | tel. 0131 527 4999 | baba.restaurant | D4*

27 THE FISHMARKET

This place right by the fishing port in Newhaven – near the final stop of the tram – serves seafood galore and really good fish and chips. The best option is to take them away (it's cheaper) and eat them sitting by the port. *Daily | 23A Pier Place | Newhaven | tel. 0131 552 8262 | thefishmarket newhaven.co.uk | I1*

28 HECTORS

The warm atmosphere at this local brings together customers of all generations to enjoy its wide range of ales on tap and the good, reasonably priced, pub food. The wings are made of cauliflower rather than chicken, sweet potatoes are served to vegetarians, and sirloin is available for meat eaters. *Daily | 47-49 Deanhaugh Street | Stockbridge | tel. 0131 343 1735 | hectorsstockbridge. co.uk | bus 24, 29 | D3*

29 MOTHER INDIA'S CAFÉ

An Asian version of tapas: this authentic Indian restaurant is right next to the *Royal Oak* (see p. 85) pub, with its live music. It offers a great base for a flavourful evening with samosas and pakoras. Last orders at 9.30pm. *Daily | 3 Infirmary Street | Old Town | tel. 0131 524 9801 | motherindia.co.uk | f-g5*

THE SCOTCH MALT WHISKY SOCIETY

A *single malt* – a whisky made with malted barley from a single distillery – is a highly prized drink. But now the market for single-cask whisky is booming: a cask is filled with 500–600 bottles' worth of whisky. It's not only the high alcohol content (around 60% ABV) that distinguishes it from other malts. Each has a distinctive taste. You can buy single-cask whiskies from the *Scotch Malt Whisky Society (28 Queens Street | New Town | smws.com)*. The origin of your bottle is shown by a number, paired with a bottle number. You will find tasting notes for the cask included with your purchase; these might include such phrases as "celebrity yurt indulgence" and "riding a duck bareback up Mount Etna". Connoisseurs can't resist the charm of the single casks – join the society to be part of it.

SHOPPING

People are more drawn to nostalgic and quirky fashion in Edinburgh than to big international brands: tartan kitsch in the Old Town, top labels in the New Town. The city's small boutiques are more exciting places than the shopping centres.

The built-up part of *Princes Street* is the place to go if you are looking for department stores, bookshops and electronics shops – and you'll still have the castle in view. Things are more high-end on the parallel *George Street* and reach their peak on chic *St Andrew Square* and *Multrees Walk*. The *Royal Mile* is in the grip of tartans, oatcakes

> You'll find all the venues in this chapter on the pull-out map

A spot of window shopping, anyone? Victoria Street is a haven of small shops

and whisky, but the *Grassmarket* – a place of execution and a slum in the Middle Ages – and the neighbouring streets, such as *Cowgate* and *Victoria Street*, are full of charming boutiques in old buildings selling fashion items and accessories made in Scotland. There are quirky designer shops in the LGBT+ district around *Broughton Street*, and the shops in *Stockbridge* on the Leith offer handmade creative items as souvenirs. Most shops are open from 9am to 6pm or 7pm from Monday to Saturday (often until 8pm on Thursdays) and from 11am to 5pm on Sundays.

WHERE EDINBURGH SHOPS

STOCKBRIDGE

Sheila Fleet Jewellery

MARCO POLO HIGHLIGHTS

★ **ST JAMES QUARTER**
Shopping mecca: 80 shops, including showrooms and food halls ➤ p. 69

★ **21ST CENTURY KILTS**
Kilts with a twist: traditional and avant-garde at the same time ➤ p. 71

★ **ARMSTRONG & SON**
A popular vintage clothes store with an illustrious past ➤ p. 71

★ **GEORGE STREET**
Edinburgh's most upmarket address is the perfect location for traditional, high-quality boutiques ➤ p. 72

★ **JOEY D**
Handbags and more for individualists ➤ p. 72

★ **SHEILA FLEET JEWELLERY**
Art inspired by the Orkney Islands: sublime interpretations of the Scottish landscape turned into jewellery by designer Sheila Fleet ➤ p. 73

★ **TARTAN WEAVING MILL**
A tartan shopping centre where the vibe is more cult than kitsch ➤ p. 74

★ **ROYAL MILE WHISKIES**
Paradise for connoisseurs: there can't be anywhere with a greater choice of whiskies than here ➤ p. 74

NEW TOWN

Queens Street

George Street

Princes Street

Princes Street

Gardens

Tartan Weaving Mill

Armstrong & Son

Fountainbridge

BROUGHTON

Leith Walk

Broughton Street

📍 Joey D ★

PRINCES, GEORGE & QUEEN STREETS

Luxury shopping in the sophisticated streets of the New Town

📍 St James Quarter ★

Leith Street

Ⓣ St Andrew Square

Calton Hill

Waterloo Place

Waverley Station 🚆

North Bridge

📍 21st Century Kilts ★

📍 Royal Mile Whiskies ★

South Bridge

AROUND THE GRASSMARKET, ROYAL MILE & COWGATE

Whisky, tartan and kilts – and charming independent boutiques

OLD TOWN

Niccison Street

Holyrood Park

SOUTHSIDE

Clerk Street

200 m
219 yd

BOOKS

WHERE TO START?

First, head for the ultimate Scottish shopping experience – on the top quarter of the **Royal Mile** *(E-H 4-5)*. You will find real Scottish couture if you turn right onto **Victoria Street**, with all kinds of exciting things down at the Grassmarket, where hat shop Fabhatrix and vintage clothing store Armstrong's await. You'll find vinyl and CDs in **Stockbridge**. For international designer labels, head to **Multrees Walk** *(multreeswalk.co.uk)* in the New Town. The **St James Quarter** brings you shopping and dining in modern, light-filled surroundings.

BOOKS

Smaller bookshops hold their own alongside the Edinburgh branch of Waterstones *(128 Princes Street | New Town | waterstones.com | D5)*. Rather than seeing floor-to-ceiling shelves of book spines, *Rare Birds Bookshop (13 Raeburn Place | Stockbridge | C3)* and *Golden Hard Books (68 St Stephen Street | Stockbridge | D3)* show their books face-on.

INSIDER TIP — Women's fiction

Rare Birds only features literature written by women. *Toppings (2 Blenheim Place | Broughton | G3)* is a sophisticated chain near Leith Walk, which displays thousands of books up to its ceiling. *Armchair Books (72-74 West Port | Old Town | e6)* does the same, but with second-hand books.

FOOD

1 CROMBIES

An exquisite butcher's shop with boar and pork "designer sausages" refined with mango, port and blue cheese. This is also the place to buy haggis for your picnic. *97–101 Broughton Street | New Town | crombiesofedinburgh.co.uk | F3*

2 I. J. MELLIS

Mellis has catered to the residents of the capital since 1993 and now has three fine cheese shops. Visitors will discover that the Scots are capable of making excellent bries and cheddars, and blue cheeses from the Isle of Arran.

INSIDER TIP — Scottish cheeses

You can taste *Clava brie, Caboc, Connage crowdie, Isle of Mull cheddar* and the strong *Lanark blue*. They also sell *Cashel blue* (Irish) and *Morbier* (French). Stock up on cheese for your picnic in Princes Street Gardens or along the Water of Leith. *mellischeese.net | 30a Victoria Street | Old Town | e5; 6 Bakers Place | Stockbridge | D3*

SHOPPING CENTRES

3 HARVEY NICHOLS

The building housing this branch of Britain's most exclusive department store, on aristocratic *St Andrew Square*, is unassuming compared with the luxurious goods hanging from the pegs and on the shelves inside. Shirts from Alexander McQueen, suits made by the most famous Saville Row tailor,

68

SHOPPING

Gieves & Hawkes, as well as the usual international designer brands. There is a restaurant with a view of the square on the upper floor. The selection of whiskies in front of it will make connoisseurs go weak at the knees: a bottle of whisky, including those of Japanese provenance, can command a four-figure price tag. Recover from the shock with sushi or in the Chocolate Lounge. Perhaps you'll have some luck in the

INSIDER TIP
Designer bargains

regular sales, for example you may be able to get a Dolce & Gabbana jacket for £100 instead of £800. *30-34 St Andrew Square | New Town | harveynichols.com | F4*

ST JAMES QUARTER ★

Before this new "lifestyle centre" had even opened in the New Town's East End in 2022, it had already provoked controversy. People said that it was ridiculous to build a consumerist temple for shopping, complete with luxury flats and a hotel, instead of affordable housing. People also found the hotel's architecture laughable: the roundish, domed exterior is encircled by an ascending bronze band; one piece of it emerges from the building, giving it the appearance of an unravelling ball of wool. Other critics argued that it looks like a dung heap.

The centre sits among the cluster of Georgian and Victorian buildings and draws attention, particularly when viewed from Calton Hill. It's not as terrible as some critics argued, but it's not well adapted to its surroundings in a World Heritage Site. Inside the shopping centre, there's a restaurant and food hall, 80 shops and lots of light, making for a relaxed place to stroll. *St James Square | stjamesquarter.com | New Town | F4*

How cheesy! Delicacies from I. J. Mellis

ART & PHOTOS

If you want to take some artwork home with you, several New Town galleries in southern *Dundas Street (E3-4)* offer enticing options. There are traditional paintings at *Harvey & Woodd (4 Dundas Street)*, and contemporary and Scottish art at *Fine Art Society (6 Dundas Street)* and the *Open Eye Gallery (Abercrombie/ Dundas intersection)*. Near Waverley

69

MARKETS & FLOWERS

It's as if vintage design were created here: second-hand dreams at Armstrong & Son

Station (F5) in the Old Town, the *Fruitmarket Gallery (45 Market Street)* offers contemporary art and the *Stills Gallery (23 Cockburn Street)* has work by Scottish photographers.

MARKETS & FLOWERS

5 BRUNTSFIELD PLACE
Would you like to spend a couple of hours in a nearby suburb with charming cafés and souvenir shops, but without any of the usual kitsch? Bruntsfield is only a 25-minute walk from the *Royal Mile* and is also easy to reach by bus. There are boutiques selling wooden toys, jewellery, novel wallpaper, shoes and children's clothing. thebruntsfield.co.uk/blog | bus 11, 15, 16, 23 | Bruntsfield | D8

6 FARMERS' MARKET
The speciality market west of the castle is the first place you should visit on a Saturday. All of the fish, cheese, pickles and vegetables on offer will whet your appetite. If you haven't had breakfast, you can even start the day here with take-away porridge. *Sat 9am–2pm | Castle Terrace | Old Town | d5*

7 RAEBURN PLACE
The main street in Stockbridge is lined with shops. This is where the locals buy their fish, get second-hand books from the Oxfam bookshop, and go to the hairdresser. The street will almost make you feel you are in a village; there's a lot to see in the shops and you'll find some real bargains – how about Dickens' *Oliver Twist* complete with a bookmark for next to nothing?

SHOPPING

The quaint *Stockbridge Market (10am–4pm)* is a good place for a second breakfast on a Sunday, or to enjoy a bowl of *paella* cooked in large pans. *Stockbridge | C3*

8 AN INDEPENDENT ZEBRA
Don't have much time to look for practical, funny or artsy homemade gifts with a Scottish touch? This shop in Stockbridge stocks many more than 50 independent Scottish designers in plenty of space. Items might include textile buttons and brooches with Highland patterns and an upcycling feel, and coasters with red-haired Highland cows. This is a skilfully designed Scottish goods shop but without the kitsch. *88–92 Raeburn Place | Stockbridge | anindependentzebra.com | C3*

> **INSIDER TIP**
> Quirky Scottish souvenirs

FASHION

9 21ST CENTURY KILTS ★
Something tailored for men who don't have tartan blood running through their veins, but fancy wearing a kilt occasionally instead of trousers: the kilts made by Howie Nicholsby give men plenty of room to stretch their legs and appear traditional and avant-garde at the same time. They can be worn with Crocs, shoes or combat boots. Kilts come in wool, leather or even PVC – and they're real eye-catchers. From around £800; make an appointment! *Royal Mile, 59 High Street | Old Town | 21stcenturykilts.com | g5*

10 ANTA
Tartan without the kitsch! Annie Stewart has been creating Scottish ceramics and fabrics for over 30 years. You won't find any better in Edinburgh. Known for using rich Highland colours. *Daily | 91 West Bow | Old Town | anta.co.uk | e5*

11 ARMSTRONG & SON ★
Second-hand clothes since 1840! Armstrong sold vintage clothes here before vintage was in vogue. Kylie Minogue and Franz Ferdinand have shopped here. There's not only Brit-retro from the past centuries but also kilts (from £50), not to forget the *sporran* – the pouch worn with a kilt. *Daily | 83 Grassmarket | Old Town | armstrongsvintage.co.uk | e5*

12 BILL BABER KNITWEAR
Knitwear designer Bill Baber describes the style of his unique label as a cross between handicraft and fashion. Linen, merino wool, cotton and silk are used in the production of pullovers, capes and jackets. They're made in an onsite workshop. *66 Grassmarket | Old Town | billbaber.com | e5*

13 KESTIN
Men's clothing from fashion designer Kestin Hare comes in high-quality materials and has a masculine, grounded charisma. Pieces include tear-resistant rugby shirts. *7 Baker's Place | Stockbridge | kestin.co | D3*

14 CORNICHE
Small boutique with intriguing, expensive individual pieces – although

FASHION

there are often good bargains to be had, too. Worth a visit just to see creations from Vivienne Westwood, Ivan Grundahl and Novemb3r. In addition, there are playful "kilt-like" trousers for men. *2 Jeffrey Street | Old Town | corniche.org.uk | g5*

15 FABHATRIX

Sherlock Holmes' deerstalker hats made of Harris tweed, and other homemade head coverings made of felt, wool or silk. Fawns Reid is the most sought-after milliner in Edinburgh. The "barely there" fascinators are also beautifully seductive. *13 Cowgatehead | Old Town | fabhatrix.com | e-f5*

INSIDER TIP: Fine fascinators

16 GEORGE STREET ★

The New Town's most aristocratic axis is the place to look for classic fashion – it's unflustered and pleasantly understated, and is an inviting place to take a stroll. You'll find respected outfitters including the American *Brooks Brothers*, yuppie Brits like the time-honoured shoemakers Church's, plus *Karen Millen* and *Jigsaw* for ladies, *Moss* with elegant suits for men, as well as the classic shirt-maker *T M Lewin*. Many shops are open until 5pm on Sunday. *New Town | edinburghgeorgestreet.co.uk | d-e4*

17 JOEY D ★

Upcycling is Joey's thing. Unique fashion items for all, made of recycled material. The designer even made Elton John chic! Clothes come with

Have your credit card at the ready for all the high-end shops on George Street

SHOPPING

the most outlandish appliqués and vivid prints, but they're always wearable. Old pieces are first cut up and then reassembled to form new creations. The handbags are the craziest item! Creative, urban, sexy – and, of course with a bit of tartan thrown in. *54 Broughton Street | New Town | F3*

> **INSIDER TIP**
> Crazy urban tartan

18 MULTREES WALK
A bit more sophisticated: this small street on the eastern side of *St Andrew Square* in the New Town has developed into the place to buy top international brands, such as Armani, Louis Vuitton, Mulberry and the like. *St Andrew Square | New Town | multreeswalk.co.uk | F4*

19 COVET
This boutique is as small as Thistle Street is narrow, but it's one of the city's top locations for handbags. Anna Somerville sells little-known European labels that can't be found outside of Edinburgh. The shop also sells four types of its own Cover Edinburgh handbag, including a clutch design, as well as scarves and jewellery. *20 Thistle Street | New Town | thoushalt covet.com | e4*

MUSIC

"Records make your life better." That's the motto of vinyl store *Thorne Records (125 Bruntsfield Place | D8)*. The smaller underground record store *Solu'shn (9 Cockburn Street | f5)* is more central. *Elvis Shakespeare (347 Leith Walk | H1)* also sells books, and *Vinyl Villains (5 Elm Row | G3)* is dedicated to metal and rock music. The Oxfam shop branch in Stockbridge *(64 Raeburn Place | C3)* is a real hit with vinyl and CD lovers, covering all genres from punk to Bob Dylan. Music shops are the best places to find info and tickets for live acts.

> **INSIDER TIP**
> Second-hand sounds

JEWELLERY & FRAGRANCES

20 SHEILA FLEET JEWELLERY ★
The jewellery designer has let the magical flair of her home on the Orkney Islands flow into her creations. For example, in her "Rowan Collection", Sheila Fleet has been inspired by the

TRADITIONALLY SCOTTISH

Scottish landscape and the reflection of the moon on the sea to create a delicate interpretation of the Highland rowan in jewellery. The changing tide, pebbles rounded by the sea and the colours of rockpools can be felt in her pieces, making them difficult to resist. *18 St Stephen Street* | *Stockbridge* | *sheilafleet.com* | *D3*

21 LE LABO
The niche perfume brand from New York has a small underground shop here. The creations are not tested on animals and are environmentally friendly, labelled with the main ingredients and the number of other ingredients included.

INSIDER TIP — A personal note

You can create your own fragrance and pick up the finished product later on. They also operate an online refill service. *46a George Street* | *New Town* | *lelabofragrances.com* | *e4*

TRADITIONALLY SCOTTISH

22 TARTAN WEAVING MILL ★
Get your dose of tartan here! You can't get past the kitsch of the *Royal Mile*, so satisfy your tartan shopping needs in this five-storey shop in the shadow of the castle. This used to be the water store for residents of the Royal Mile, but today it's run by the *Geoffrey Tailor Kiltmaker* (which also has two shops on the Royal Mile). You can learn about the entire industrial process, from shearing sheep to creating the final product. You can even have your picture taken in a kilt. Nobody leaves without a long-lasting, functional or ornamental gem. The high-quality cashmere scarves, decorated in the LGBT+ rainbow tartan, are special.

INSIDER TIP — LGBT+ tartan scarves

The silly yet funny mini bagpipes don't cost a lot. *Daily* | *555 Castle Hill* | *Old Town* | *thetartanweavingmill.co.uk* | *e5*

23 BAGPIPES GALORE
At this shop opposite the famous Festival Theatre, you can buy bagpipes (or get them repaired). They sell small pipes for beginners and for travelling, and highland bagpipes for experienced players. *8a Nicolson Street* | *Old Town* | *g6*

24 HAWICO
The lightweight, expensive goats' wool comes from China and Mongolia, but it has been processed in the small town of Hawick in the south of Scotland since 1874. This is a luxury knitwear brand whose goods are known worldwide. *71 Grassmarket* | *Old Town* | *hawico.com/stores* | *e5*

25 KINLOCH ANDERSON
An institution: Highland dress at its best has been sold here since 1868. This is a serious kilt shop for connoisseurs and and anyone who wants to learn. Take the plunge. *4 Dock Street* | *Leith* | *kinlochanderson.com* | *L1–2*

26 ROYAL MILE WHISKIES ★
It is said that this shop has more than 300 kinds of whisky in stock and you are welcome to taste them. However,

SHOPPING

Discover how tartan and kilts are made at the Tartan Weaving Mill

it makes more sense to be completely sober and let the imaginative labels and names inspire you when you make your choice. *379 High Street | Old Town | royalmilewhiskies.com | f5*

27 SCOTTISH DESIGNER KNITWEAR

This canyon of a street in the Old Town might appear rather gloomy, but the colours and vivacity of the fashions designed by Joyce Forsyth will make you forget it. Knitwear to clothe the lady with a taste for unusual patterns from head to toe. *42 Candlemaker Row | Old Town | scottishdesignerknitwear.co.uk | f6*

28 SCOTTISH WHISKY HERITAGE CENTRE

A tour through the history of whisky will put you in the right mood to buy a bottle – and almost 280 kinds are on sale here. The shop near the castle also sees whisky as a form of entertainment. Tours are available from £21. *354 Castlehill | Old Town | scotchwhiskyexperience.co.uk | e5*

29 THE WHISKY SHOP

The cosiest whisky shop in Edinburgh is steeped in atmosphere. An estimated 500 labels are stored in this relatively small space, including their own whisky brand: Glenkeir Treasures, whose taste is reminiscent, apparently, of beach bonfires and fruit.

INSIDER TIP: Taste of Scotland

The new showroom in the St James Quarter is like a temple. The 200ml and 500ml bottles filled directly from the cask are not off-the-shelf items, and they're not cheap either. *28 Victoria Street | Old Town | whiskyshop.com | e-f5*

NIGHTLIFE

Edinburgh's many charms are also on show at night, when people head to its countless cinemas, pubs and small clubs. On the whole, the atmosphere is more lounge than loud, more folk and jazz than rock.

First things first: the evening usually gets under way either in one of the many cocktail bars in the New Town or with a pint in the pub. Beer tends to be more popular than wine, but if you prefer wine, the area between Raeburn Place and Circus Place in *Stockbridge* will meet your requirements.

> You'll find all the venues in this chapter on the pull-out map 📖

Jamming with the locals: folk music in Sandy Bell's

At the busy *Tollcross* corner the partygoers are often younger, but this is also where you will find the best theatre. *George Street* has a reputation for being posh, and the queues outside the clubs are longer here. The pub scene around the *Grassmarket* in the Old Town promises a lively start to the evening.

The old harbour area in ★ *Leith* has developed into a popular place to go out. You can get the tram here from the city centre, and can also take the tram to the nearby port of Newhaven, where there are good fish restaurants.

WHERE EDINBURGH GOES OUT

MARCO POLO HIGHLIGHTS

★ **LEITH**
The old port has become a hip place to go out ➤ p. 77

★ **CAFÉ ROYAL OYSTER BAR**
Sophisticated drinks and extravagant Victorian-pub elegance ➤ p. 82

★ **THE VOODOO ROOMS**
Magnificently flamboyant event venue and cocktail bar ➤ p. 84

★ **CABARET VOLTAIRE**
First-rate music cellar with a dance club; the best of its kind ➤ p. 85

★ **SANDY BELL'S**
Daily folk music sessions with local and international stars ➤ p. 86

★ **FESTIVAL THEATRE**
Edinburgh's top theatre for plays, opera and dance ➤ p. 86

NEW TOWN
Sip cocktails in chic venues and queue for popular, stylish clubs

LEITH
Buzzing eating and entertainment hub between The Shore and Commercial Street

OLD TOWN
Classic pub scene: beer on tap, folk fiddles and jazz sessions

- Leith
- Café Royal Oyster Bar
- The Voodoo Rooms
- Cabaret Voltaire
- Festival Theatre
- Sandy Bell's

NEWHAVEN
BROUGHTON
ABBEYHILL
OLD TOWN
SOUTHSIDE
Holyrood Park

400 m / 437 yd

BARS, PUBS & CAFÉS

WHERE TO START?

A cocktail in the exuberant and down-to-earth Old Town, for example at the **Dragonfly** (p. 84), is a good place to start your evening. The liveliest nightlife awaits between the **Grassmarket** and **Cowgate**. Fans of the more fashionable, funky and chic New Town style navigate towards the area between **St Andrew Square** and **George Square**. **Broughton** has a lively gay scene in the area known as the *Pink Triangle*. Lovers of folk will head to the **Royal Oak** (p. 85) for a midnight jam session.

BARS, PUBS & CAFÉS

1 THE BAILIE BAR

The island bar turns a full 360 degrees, and there are probably at least the same number of drinks served here. A cosy pub with a cellar, The Bailie attracts everyone from students and bankers to people who come to watch sport on TV. It's in a trendy area, near the bridge over the Leith, and serves good bar food *(£)*. *Daily 11am–midnight | 2–4 St Stephen Street | Stockbridge | ▯ D3*

2 LE DI-VIN

This much-loved wine bar celebrates the medieval French-Scottish alliance known as the *Auld Alliance* with a mural in the style of *The Last Supper*, featuring famous French and Scottish guests, among them General de Gaulle and Sean Connery. Set in a former nunnery, it's an atmospheric gem with 30 wines available by the glass, located between the West End and Dean Village. A Paolozzi beermat is a nice souvenir of the beer brewed to honour the Scottish artist Eduardo Paolozzi, whose work is exhibited in the nearby *Scottish National Gallery of Modern Art.* Upstairs you can eat contemporary French dishes at the equally atmospheric *La P'tite Folie*, which offers a two-course set lunch. *Both closed Sun | 9 Randolph Place | New Town | ▯ C5*

> **INSIDER TIP**
> For the sake of art

3 STARBAR

A small neighbourhood pub with a big heart, even for thirsty tourists who have ended up here by accident. It may be located in a very posh area, but it's a simple spot. The atmosphere is very lively and you can play table football, put a song on the jukebox (with the likes of Status Quo, Kate Bush and Queen) and look at the skeleton on display. There is also a small beer garden. A good place for curious people who love to talk. *Daily until midnight | 1 Northumberland Place | New Town | ▯ E3*

4 CUMBERLAND BAR

A tasteful neighbourhood pub in a tasteful area, with cosy rooms and a beer garden for mild summer evenings. It's also cosy in winter. They serve roasts on Sundays. *Daily | 1–3 Cumberland Street | New Town | ▯ E3*

NIGHTLIFE

So much choice: around 400 types of beer are served in Brauhaus

5 THE BANSHEE LABYRINTH

The labyrinthine and subterranean Banshee has three bars and a horror theme – there's even a banshee that haunts the place. There are seven crypt-like rooms, jukeboxes, a dancefloor complete with pole, and a small cinema for classics, comedy, poetry slams and zombie parties. Excellent DJ sets and live gigs, and there are even cosy corners for a "candlelight burger". *Daily | 29-35 Niddry Street | thebansheelabyrinth.com | Old Town | D f5*

INSIDER TIP Bring on the zombies!

6 BENNET'S BAR

Wonderful Victorian decor, including a "jug bar" where women could be separate from men, and plenty of brass, wood and stained-glass windows (this also makes it a good place to visit during the day). It's next to the *King's Theatre*, which means that the bar is packed after performances. It also screens rugby. More locals than tourists. *Daily until 1am | 8 Leven Street | Old Town | D D7*

7 BRAUHAUS

A small, popular beer bar with a nod to Bavaria and 400 types of beer. It's not easy to make the right choice, but the friendly staff behind the bar will be able to help you. Have something small to eat while you're trying the brew – maybe a pretzel? Young crowd, students and football on TV. *Daily until midnight | 105-107 Lauriston Place | Old Town | D D6*

BARS, PUBS & CAFÉS

8 CAFÉ ROYAL OYSTER BAR ★
Established in 1826, this is probably the most magnificent bar in town, with its listed Victorian furnishings. The bar sits in the middle, and walls are decorated with tile paintings from 1886 showing prominent inventors – Benjamin Franklin, Isaac Newton, Michael Faraday, James Watt, and so on – surveying the crowd of locals and tourists. Try the Shetland mussels from the kitchen of the attached Oyster Bar. The *Guildford Arms* on the same street (nos 1–5) is rather similar. *Daily usually until 11pm, sometimes until midnight | 19 West Register Street | New Town | f4*

9 THE DOME
This former bank was built in 1847 and looks like an ornate, domed temple. Today, it's a nightclub, restaurant and bar, with a grandiose façade on George Street and a rear entrance with a garden terrace on to bustling Rose Street. Well-off locals meet here under the chandeliers hanging from the 15m-high ceilings for their *latte*, lunch or dinner. Confidently chic. *Daily 10am–midnight | 14 George Street | New Town | e4*

10 HALFWAY HOUSE
This place may no longer be independently run and may only sell microwaved pies, but it's still a hidden meeting spot and top pub choice for locals and insiders, near the rear exit of Waverley Station. The smallest pub in Edinburgh is

INSIDER TIP: Small pub, big atmosphere

Can I open a Prosecco account? The Dome used to be a bank

NIGHTLIFE

found on a typical steep stairway. Despite its size, it still has four ales on tap and 30 different malts on offer. *Daily from 11am | 24 Fleshmarket Close | Old Town | ▢ f5*

11 HANGING BAT
More of a brewery with stools than a pub, and it calls itself a beer café. Besides an exhaustive range of 150 really special beers, there are also a few gins and wines, but rarely lagers. Draught beer isn't offered in pints, but in smaller glasses (425ml) for enhanced freshness and enjoyment. Hotdogs and burgers are served as an accompaniment. *Daily until midnight | 133 Lothian Road | Old Town | ▢ D6*

INSIDER TIP: Great beer but no pints

12 HECTOR'S
The cosy corners of this quality pub, with candles on the tables, attract middle-class patrons in the New Town. There's modern music, including DJ sets at the weekend. Excellent Saturday brunch, a pub quiz on a Sunday. Booking recommended. *Daily until 11pm | 47–49 Deanhaugh Street | Stockbridge | tel. 0131 343 1735 | ▢ C3*

13 JUNIPER
A popular place to come for a glass of prosecco, a gin and tonic or cocktails in the early evening. The view from the window sweeps over Princes Street to the Old Town. *Daily noon–11pm | 20 Princes Street | New Town | ▢ f4*

14 TEUCHTERS LANDING
A balmy summer evening and nowhere to go? Catch a tram to Leith and grab a table in the popular beer garden on the harbour, behind the cosy, upmarket pub-restaurant *A Room in Leith*. The building is a bit difficult to find; it's one of the remnants of the former customs and ferry port. It's on the cycle route from George V Park in New Town to Leith. Get a Scots language lesson with your drink: *hawf 'n' hawf* means "half a pint of beer plus a single malt dram". *Daily 10am–1am | 1c Dock Place | Leith | teuchtersbar.co.uk | tram: Port of Leith, bus 16, 32, 34, night bus 16 Sandport Street | ▢ L1*

INSIDER TIP: What's in a name?

15 SHEEP HEID INN ▶
The oldest pub in Scotland (1360) is known for its quaint atmosphere and tasty food (it's a popular place for Sunday lunch). From Parliament, it's a pleasurable walk *(3km/1 hr)* around Arthur's Seat, no matter which direction. It's all very relaxing: the village of Duddingston, a bit like a mountain village; the romantic loch; the pub and Dr Neil's Garden (see also Discovery Tour p.113) *Daily until 11pm | 43–45 The Causeway | Duddingston | thesheepheidedinburgh.co.uk | bus 12 Holyrood High School | ▢ L7*

16 ST BERNHARD'S BAR
They only play vinyl in this cosy pub, which does a great line in cocktails as well as beers! The steep steps lead to a

CLUBS

See and be seen in dazzling surroundings: The Voodoo Rooms

second bar with homely private rooms, called Speakeasy. *Daily until midnight or 1am | 10 Rayburn Place | Stockbridge | C3*

CLUBS

17 DRAGONFLY

The ageing top dog among the old-school cocktail bars. In keeping with the Old Town, it's small, not very upmarket but warm, with skilled staff. It has cult status and phenomenal cocktails. *Wed–Sun until 1am | 52 West Port | Old Town | dragonflycocktailbar.com | e6*

18 THE VOODOO ROOMS ★

A place with style. With bombastic Victorian design, the trendiest lounge, cocktail and event bar is located above the more exclusive Café Royal Oyster Bar (p. 82). It offers drinks, live bands and theatrical performances. There's a chill-out salon with subtle lighting, a magnificent ballroom and a space with an opium-den vibe. ☛ You can have an unpretentious pre-theatre dinner here and bar snacks are available until closing time. *Daily until 1am | admission from £ 6 | 19a West Register Street | New Town | thevoodoorooms.com | f4*

CINEMAS

Although the people of Edinburgh like going to the cinema, and the city would provide a great setting for films,

NIGHTLIFE

20 THE SCOTSMAN PICTUREHOUSE

This cosy boutique cinema is part of the revered Scotsman Hotel. A visit here is like travelling back in time, with its 48 seats fitted with tables and retro-style lights. It shows a nice mix of new blockbusters and classics that haven't been seen on the big screen in a while. *Admission from £13 | 20 North Bridge | Old Town | scotsmanpicturehouse.co.uk | f5*

LIVE MUSIC

21 CABARET VOLTAIRE ★

The city's most popular venue for live gigs. The club under the Old Town, with its multiple stages and dance-floors, doesn't close until 3am. Often plays indie-electro music. Weekend tip: Japanese street food. Interesting from 7pm onwards. *Fri, Sat 7pm–3am | admission free or up to £20 | 36 Blair Street | Old Town | thecabaretvoltaire.com | f5*

22 THE BONGO CLUB

Calling all night owls. For 25 years, this has been a place for people who like to leave the house just before midnight for a night out and who like their gigs to be outside the mainstream. Intimate, excellent atmosphere. *Mon-Sat 11pm–3am| 66 Cowgate | Old Town | thebongoclub.co.uk | f5*

23 ROYAL OAK

A spot with cult status for music purists and folk fans, but it's still a hidden secret, with a good restaurant next to it.

comparatively few are made here. Most of the cult film *Trainspotting* was actually shot in Glasgow. The cinema programme changes on Fridays. You can find out what's showing online.

19 CAMEO PICTUREHOUSE

This listed art house cinema is one of Scotland's oldest cinemas still in use and is a venue for the *Edinburgh International Film Festival*. Cinema 1 is the most charming of its three auditoriums. Comfortable seating with elegant seating and ample legroom. Inviting bar – drinks can be taken into the auditorium. *Admission from £11 | 38 Home Street | Old Town | picturehouses.com | D7*

85

LGBT+

During the day, this is about as empty and austere as a pub can be. But during the evening the two small bars on the ground floor and in the basement fill up and the air vibrates with the sound of strings, bows and voices. It features folk music, with some unique performances. If you talk during the gig, you'll be thrown out! It's an alternative gem on the live music scene. If you're hungry, enjoy *samosas*, *pakoras* and tapas-style curries in the first-rate *Mother India's Café (see p. 63)* next door. *Daily 3pm–2am | 1 Infirmary Street | Old Town | g5*

INSIDER TIP — Folk music: Scottish soul

24 SANDY BELL'S ⭐ 🏴

Typical, simple pub that doesn't serve food, near Greyfriars Kirkyard. It really comes alive in the afternoon and evening when local and international folk music stars get together for a jam session. Fiddles, guitars, singing: Celtic lifestyle at its best. *Daily noon–1am, 2–3 sessions | 25 Forrest Road | Old Town | f6*

LGBT+

Edinburgh's *pink triangle* is located in the New Town between Broughton Street and the Leith Walk end of Princes Street *(F-G 2-3)*. It's not only the LGBT+ scene that dines and parties here, and the scene is booming.

CC Blooms (daily 1pm–3am | 23 Greenside Place) is both a restaurant and party location. Next door, the two-storey *Habana (daily 1pm–1am | 22 Greenside Place)* invites you in for a drink; *Regent Bar (daily 4pm–midnight | 2 Montrose Terrace)* is a sophisticated gay pub with no loud music or dancefloor.

Further information available at: *black-kilt-tours.org/edinburgh-gay-bars*

THEATRE & CLASSICAL MUSIC

25 FESTIVAL THEATRE ⭐

The most prestigious theatre in Edinburgh, and not only during the festival. The premises are a stylish mixture of an old theatre building and modern glass architecture. The Art Nouveau/Beaux Arts auditorium, with its impressive decor, can seat about 1,900. Modern dance, opera, drama – all the top names perform here. The café is more modern, and serves a delicious lunch. *Admission £15–£110 | 13–29 Nicolson Street | Old Town | capitaltheatres.com | g6*

26 KING'S THEATRE

A theatre out of an old picture book: wood, marble and gold leaf create an elegant setting for plays, musicals, comedies and opera. There are pubs next door so you can knock back a quick pint during the interval. This is where Sean Connery made his first appearance as an actor. *Admission from £20 | 2 Leven Street | Old Town | capitaltheatres.com | D7*

27 PLAYHOUSE

A large auditorium on Calton Hill with 3,000 spaces. Global stars have performed here, including Steely Dan,

NIGHTLIFE

The Festival Theatre: chic home of theatre, ballet and opera

Tom Waits and Katie Melua. It also features musicals and is a venue for well-known British stand-up comedians. *Admission from £25 | 18–22 Greenside Place | New Town | playhousetheatre.com | D G3*

28 ROYAL LYCEUM THEATRE

The classics and – occasionally – contemporary plays are performed in a beautiful Victorian building dating from 1883. It is even said that a ghost haunts the gallery. As many as eight plays are staged annually, making the Royal Lyceum, in its own words, the largest dramatic theatre in Scotland. *Admission from £25 | Grindlay Street | Old Town | lyceum.org.uk | D D6*

29 TRAVERSE THEATRE

The centre for contemporary Scottish theatre. Fans of these types of performances will find what they are looking for on the stage in the cellar; those who want to sample Edinburgh's modern social scene should also visit the Traverse Bar Café. It's a popular Festival Fringe meeting point. *Free or up to £25 | 10 Cambridge Street | Old Town | traverse.co.uk | D D5*

30 USHER HALL

This circular theatre is the venue for the most important classical concerts during the Edinburgh International Festival. At other times, there are concerts with symphony orchestras, jazz stars and rock bands. The main organ is a real treasure. *From £25 | Castle Steps/Lothian Road | Old Town | usherhall.co.uk | D D5–6*

ACTIVE & RELAXED

Chill out around the castle: West Princes Street Gardens

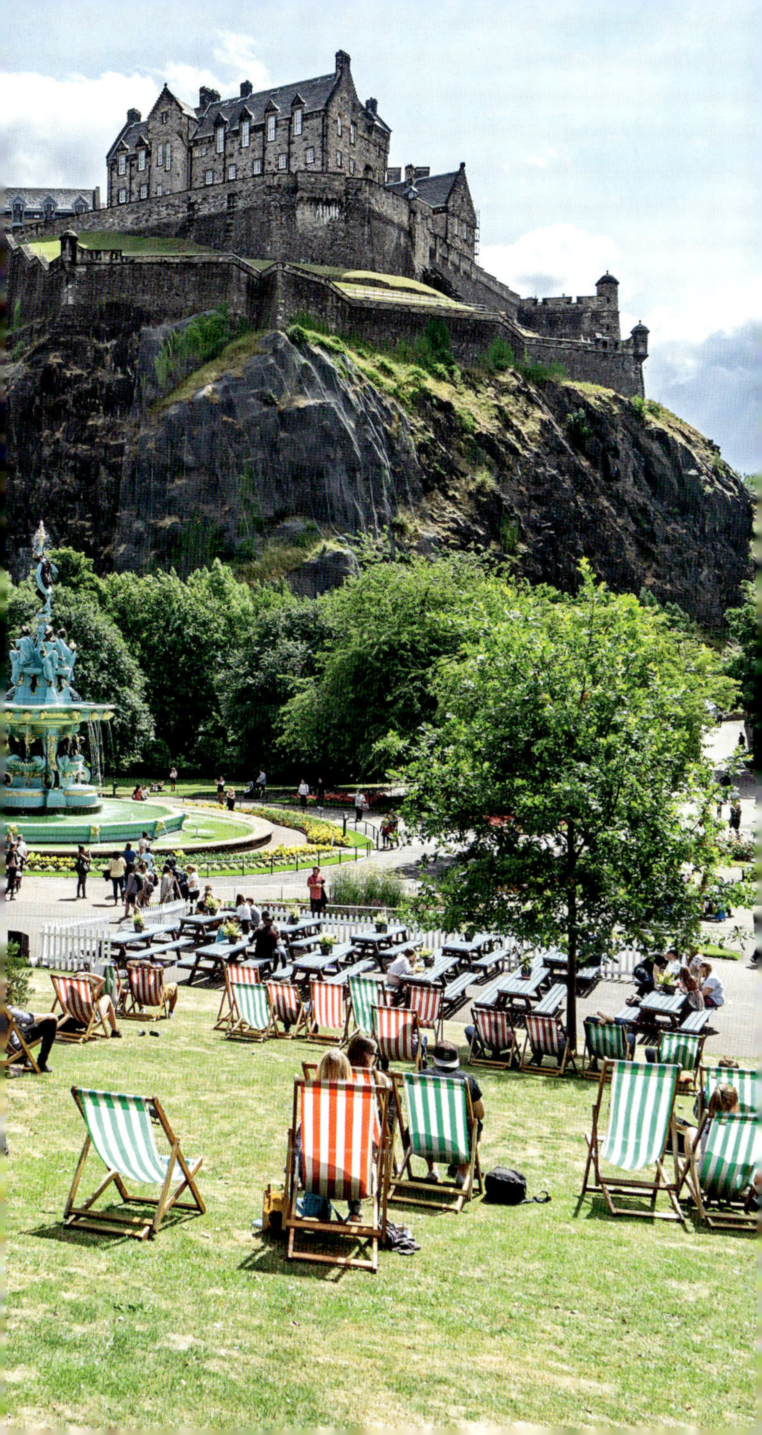

SPORT & WELLNESS

ABSEILING & CLIMBING
Abseiling 50m off the Forth Rail Bridge *(£21 | chss.org.uk)* in June and October not only gives you a huge kick, but also supports Chest, Heart & Stroke Scotland, a charity helping people with lung or heart conditions and stroke patients.

Ratho is home to one of the largest indoor climbing arenas: *Edinburgh International Climbing Arena (Mon–Fri 10am–10pm, Sat, Sun 9am–6pm | from £10.99 | South Platt Hill | Newbridge | tel. 0131 333 6333 | edinburghleisure.co.uk/venues | Airport tram, then a few minutes by taxi)* is great for lead climbing and bouldering.

CURLING
Like boules, but on ice. Curling combines stretches, whipping around on ice without ice skates, burning calories, having fun with your friends, and using tactics more typical of a board game. The sport was invented in Scotland 500 years ago and its popularity is booming. ==From October to March, Edinburgh residents enjoy indoor curling at the *Murrayfield Curling Rink*== *(see website for available times | 2-hr taster course £14 | 13A Riversdale Crescent | tel. 0131 337 4242 | edinburghcurling.co.uk/try-curling, trycurling.com | tram Murrayfield Stadium)*.

INSIDER TIP: Scotland's cult sport

CYCLING
Cyclists can enjoy a 75km network of cycle routes along stretches of former railway line away from the roads. Use the signposts and a map of the network *(innertubemap.com, edinburgh.cyclestreets.net)* to guide you. Most of the route is flat, but the wonderful journey around *Arthur's Seat*

Edinburgh offers some fun routes for off-road cyclists

undulates quite a bit. The Innocent Rail Tunnel (a good 500m stretch) is interesting when you cycle from Holyrood Park to Leith, or even Portobello. The routes away from the roads have been very well signposted since 2022.

It's worth bringing your own bike with you. Otherwise, you can rent one *(from £28/day, e-bike from £45)* or you can book a sightseeing tour *(edinburghbiketours.co.uk)*. Find more information at *cyclingedinburgh.org.uk*.

SPAS & MORE

Everyone needs pure relaxation from time to time, and there are several exquisite feel-good oases in the city's hotels. The best is *One Spa (Mon–Fri 6.30am–10pm, Sat, Sun 7am–9pm | £80 for 3 hrs, with pool, gym and sauna | 8 Conference Square | onespa. com)* on the roof of the five-star *Sheraton Grand* hotel: the facilities include Turkish and aroma baths, massages, exercise machines, saunas, rainforest-scented showers and a salt-water outdoor infinity pool with a view over the city.

WALKING & JOGGING

Just walking up and down the steps and steep streets of the Old Town should take care of average fitness requirements.

The hilly profile of the city offers many interesting places for runners: an early-morning run through the still deserted *Princes Street Gardens* below the castle in the *Old Town* is a wonderful experience. The beautiful landscape can be enjoyed on runs along the *Water of Leith* and, in particular, up to *Arthur's Seat* from the lower end of Royal Mile.

FESTIVALS & EVENTS

JANUARY
25 January: Robert Burns' birthday is celebrated in restaurants on *Burns Night (edinburghguide.com/festival/burnsnight)* with haggis and whisky, and recitals of his verses.

APRIL
Around Easter: the two-week *International Science Festival (sciencefestival.co.uk)* focuses on technology and science.
30 April: The *Beltane Fire Festival (beltane.org)* is a Celtic mega-party on Calton Hill. More than 12,000 people welcome in the summer with bonfires and drums.
Last week April–first week May: The *TradFest (edinburghtradfest.com)* celebrates Scottish culture.

MAY
Late May: The *Imaginate Festival (imaginate.org.uk/festival)* is Britain's largest theatre festival for children and young people, but there are also many adults in the audience.
Late May/early June: Running for four days, the *Hidden Door Festival (hiddendoorblog.org)* is a colourful, fun theatre and music event in Leith Theatre and State Cinema.

JUNE
Early June: The 11-day *Edinburgh Festival of Cycling (edfoc.org.uk)*.
Mid-June: The four-day *Royal Highland Show (royalhighlandshow.org)*, held near the airport, is Scotland's largest agricultural show.
Second half June: the 12-day *Edinburgh International Film Festival (edfilmfest.org.uk)* draws many stars.

JULY
Mid-July: The *Edinburgh Jazz & Blues Festival (edinburghjazzfestival.com)* lasts ten days.

Tickets for the Military Tattoo are always in high demand

AUGUST/SEPTEMBER

August is when it all happens in Edinburgh, with a stunning collection of events.

Three weeks from early Aug: The *Royal Edinburgh Military Tattoo (edintattoo.co.uk)*, with the castle as its backdrop, is the most spectacular military-band festival in the world.

Three weeks from early Aug: the *Edinburgh International Festival (eif.co.uk)*, with a classic programme, and the ★ *Edinburgh Festival Fringe (edfringe.com, freefestival.co.uk)* with theatre and comedy, are two of the world's largest cultural events.

Two weeks mid-Aug: The *Edinburgh International Book Festival (edbookfest.co.uk)*, with more than 800 events.

Four weeks Aug/Sept: The *Edinburgh Art Festival (edinburghartfestival.com)* takes place in the city's museums and galleries.

SEPTEMBER

Early Sept: The multicultural carnival *Edinburgh Mela (FB: TheEdMela)* comes to Leith.

OCTOBER

Last week Oct: Scottish people love telling stories, and celebrate this at the *Scottish International Storytelling Festival (sisf.org.uk)*.

DECEMBER

Mid-late Dec: *Edinburgh Christmas (edinburgh-christmas.com)* is Britain's largest Christmas market, with an ice-skating rink; held in Princes Street Gardens.

29 Dec-1 Jan: The New Year's celebration is known as *Hogmanay (edinburghhogmanay.org)*. The highlight is the New Year's Eve street party (admission free!), where tens of thousands celebrate on the streets across the whole city.

SLEEP WELL

SLEEP ON THE WATER
Fingal (Alexandra Dock | tel. 0131 357 5000 | fingal.co.uk | bus 16 Bernard Street | £££ | Leith | L1), a former lighthouse service ship, made a home for itself in Leith harbour in 2019. Members of the former *Royal Yacht Britannia* crew run this floating five-star boutique retreat, with its 23 cabins and suites. There is also a restaurant and bar with floor-to-ceiling windows, where you may be treated to the dulcet tones of the grand piano in the ballroom.

A TOUCH OF MARY STUART
Enchanting! It's said that the Lamb family entertained Mary Stuart at *Lamb's House (11 Waters' Close | tel. 0131 467 7777 | lambspavilion.com | tram Port of Leith or bus 22 The Shore | £££ | Leith | L2)* after she came to claim the Scottish throne in 1561. The current proprietor is also the Icelandic honorary consul in Edinburgh, which is why the Icelandic flag flies in front of the restored home. Set in flawless Renaissance-inspired shrub gardens, the Pavilion is a cottage that sleeps six – try to book it for at least a long weekend. The typical Scottish box bed for two people is a real highlight.

JEKYLL & HYDE AS A BEDTIME STORY
The author Robert Louis Stevenson (1850–94) lived here from the age of six; today guests can sleep in *Stevenson House (17 Heriot Row | tel. 0131 556 1896 | stevenson-house.co.uk | ££ | New Town | D4)*, which is almost the same now as it was then. The only double room has an antique four-poster bed, while the breakfast is more in keeping with our times and includes sourdough bread and muesli. The Georgian townhouse also has two single rooms.

Rocked gently by the waves: the *Fingal* hotel ship

B&B AT CALTON HILL

Anyone who spends the night at Dave and Tokes's *Brunton Bothy (Brunton Place | tel. 07875 333539 | FB: bruntonbothy | ££ | New Town | H3)* is sure to fall in love with the way they have styled their small B&B (by the way, calling it "Bothy" is ironic as it means a rural hut!). You'll feel like a guest of honour without being fussed over, and their tips on things to do are worth their weight in gold!

LIVELY OUTSIDE, COSY INSIDE

You can stay between the castle and Greyfriars Kirkyard without any ghostly comings and goings. Outside the thick walls of this small, well-appointed flat on *Candlemaker Row (48/1 Candlemaker Row | tel. 0131 538 0352 | candlemaker-row-view-of-edinburgh-castle.booked.net | £££ | Old Town | F6)*, you will be right in midst of the hustle and bustle of the Old Town. Inside, it's cosy and quiet under the low ceilings.

ALL ABOARD

There's another hotel ship in Leith. *Ocean Mist (17 cabins | 14 Shore | tel. 0131 322 3330 | oceanmistleith.com | £££ | Leith | L1)* is moored at The Shore, the district of Leith that's full of pubs and restaurants.

INSIDER TIP: Sleep in a nightlife hub

The steamship was built as a minesweeper 100 years ago, but later found itself serving as a luxury yacht. It has three types of cabin and a great bar. A little less luxurious and more affordable than *Fingal* (p. 94).

DISCOVERY TOURS

Want to get under the skin of the city? Then our discovery tours are the ideal guide – they provide advice on which sights to visit, tips on where to stop for that perfect holiday snap, a choice of the best places to eat and drink, and suggestions for fun activities.

The dream view from Calton Hill: Dugald Stewart Monument and Princes Street

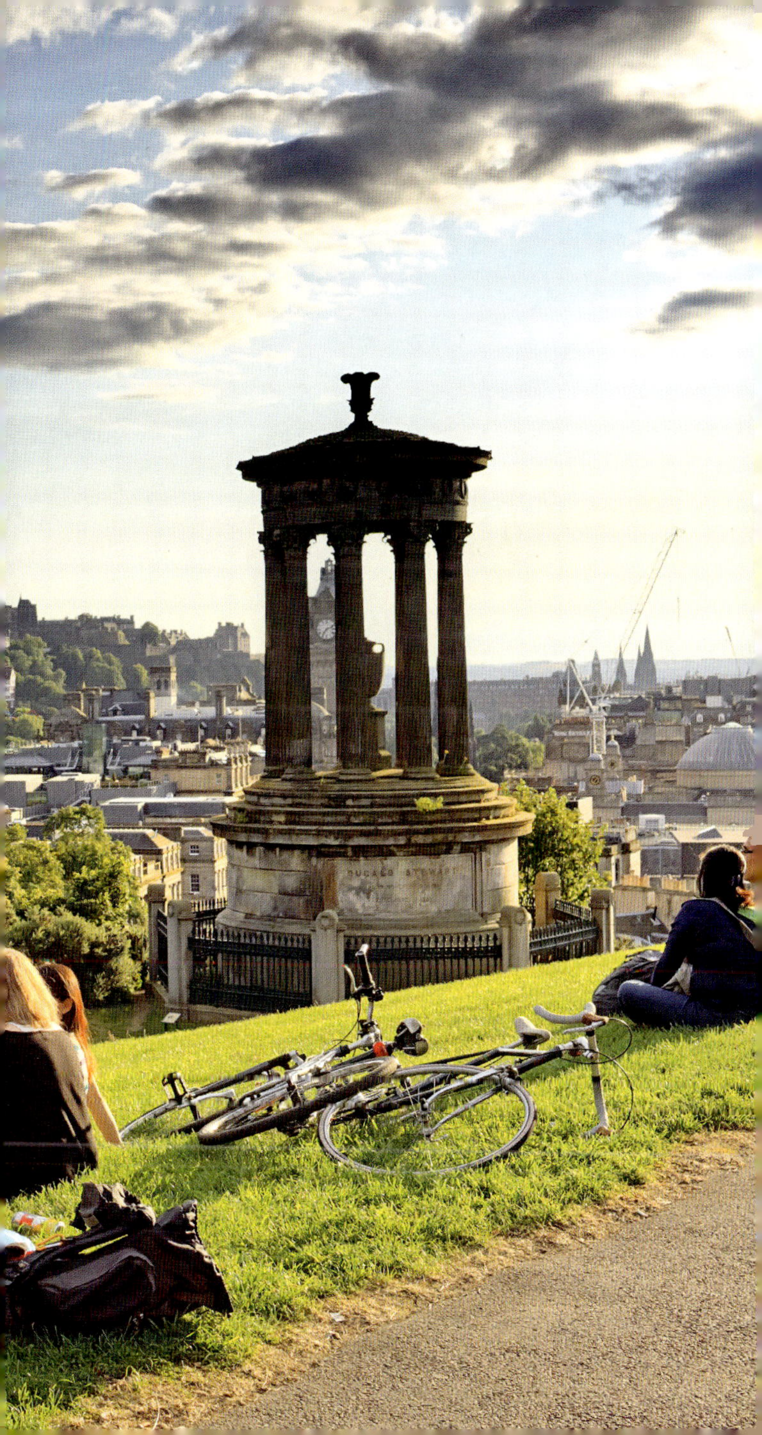
DUGALD STEWART

DISCOVERY TOURS OVERVIEW

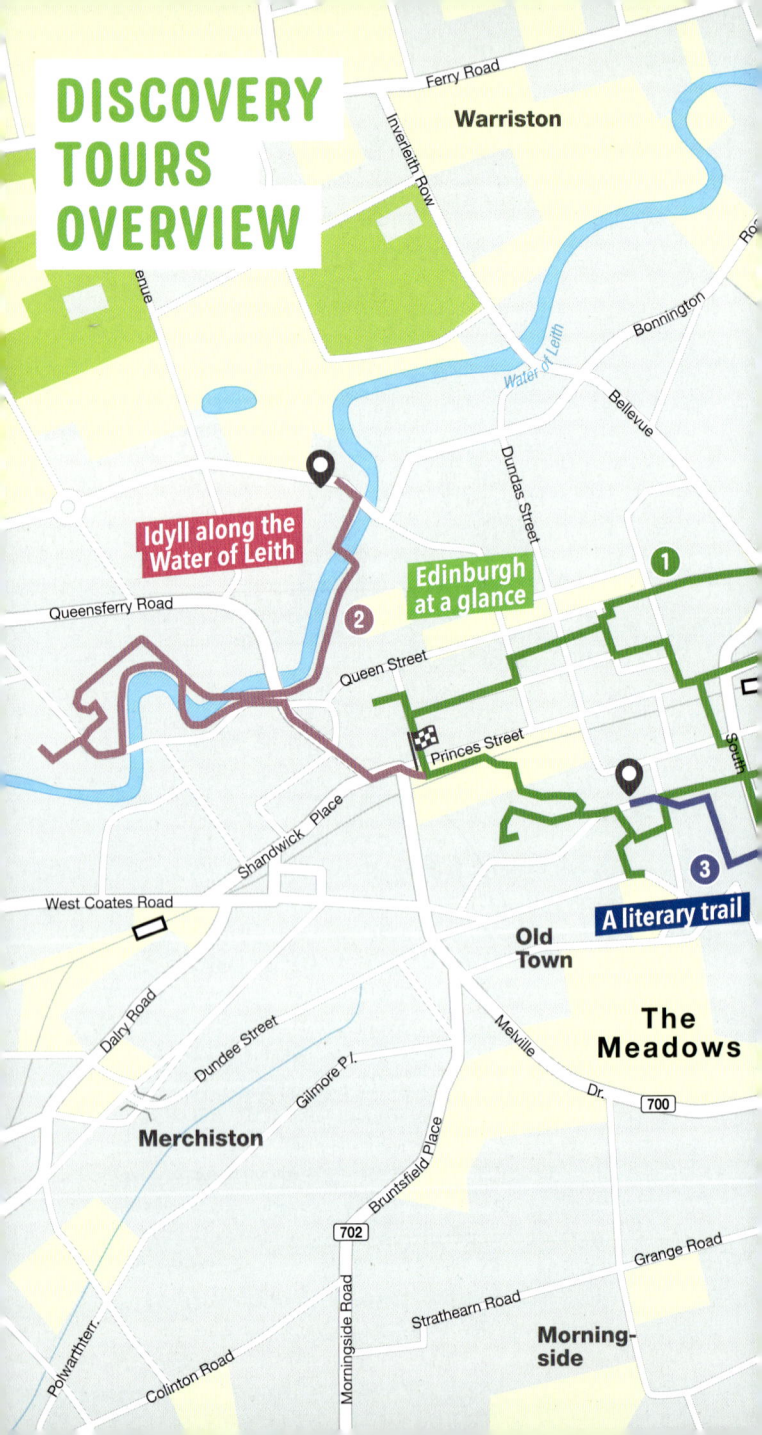

- **Idyll along the Water of Leith** ❷
- **Edinburgh at a glance** ❶
- **A literary trail** ❸

Warriston · Ferry Road · Inverleith Row · Bonnington · Bellevue · Water of Leith · Dundas Street · Queensferry Road · Queen Street · Princes Street · Shandwick Place · West Coates Road · Dalry Road · Dundee Street · Gilmore Pl. · Merchiston · Melville Dr. · Bruntsfield Place · Old Town · The Meadows · Polwarthterr. · Colinton Road · Morningside Road · Strathearn Road · Grange Road · Morningside

700 · 702

Over the volcano

Holyrood Park

Arthur's Seat

④

Areas
- Restalrig
- Northfield
- Newington
- Prestonfield

Water
- Dunsapie Loch
- Duddingston Loch

Streets
- Salamander Street
- Pilrig Street
- Leith Walk
- Restalrig Road
- Lochend Road
- Easter Road
- Sleigh Drive
- London Road
- Regent Road
- Canongate
- Pleasance
- Queen's Drive
- Duddingston Low Road
- Newington Road
- Dalkeith Road
- Peffermill Road

900 | 199 | 1 | 7 | 701

🟢 EDINBURGH AT A GLANCE

- Go shopping and explore the chic New Town
- Enjoy dreamy views of the city's hills
- Come face to face with the soul of Scotland in the Old Town

📍 Valvona & Crolla	🏁 Royal Oak
→ 9.6km	🚶 1 day (3 hrs total walking time)

To pack: A hip flask to fill up at ❽ **The Whisky Shop** in case you fancy a dram later on.
Important tip: ❶ **Valvona & Crolla** opens at 8.30am during the week.

❶ Valvona & Crolla

❷ Scottish National Portrait Gallery

❸ St Andrew Square

❹ George Street

FIRST BREAKFAST, THEN SOME ART

Start your tour with a cappuccino and Italian-style breakfast in the hip Italian café ❶ Valvona & Crolla ➤ p. 56 in the New Town, surrounded by Georgian and neoclassical architecture. After your morning feast, *turn to the south, with Calton Hill ➤ p. 44 on your left. Walk along Leith Walk and, at York Place, head west to the* ❷ Scottish National Portrait Gallery ➤ p. 44. Behind the neo-Gothic façade, you will see a *Who's Who* of historic and contemporary Scottish VIPs captured in paintings, photographs and even videos.

WINDOW SHOPPING AND A JOURNEY THROUGH TIME

Two blocks further south, ❸ St Andrew Square ➤ p. 64 *opens up at the end of a small side street on the other side of Queen Street.* The large department store **Harvey Nichols ➤ p. 68** and the huge **St James Quarter ➤ p. 69** have both become magnets for shoppers in the East End. Now *wander westwards* while window shopping along ❹ George Street ➤ p. 72, with its rows of brand-name stores. In dramatic contrast, you'll notice the skyline of the medieval Old Town on your left. In front of you is the Georgian Charlotte

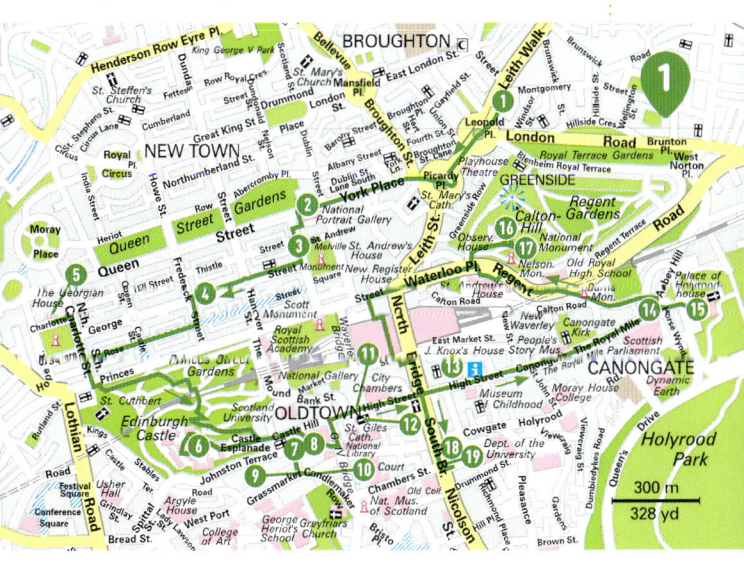

DISCOVERY TOURS

Square, designed by Robert Adams in 1791 and now home to the head of the Scottish government, who lives at no. 6. The National Trust for Scotland owns no. 7, running it as a museum called ❺ Georgian House ➤ p. 44. Immerse yourself in the perfectly restored 200-year-old home of a wealthy family.

❺ Georgian House

FROM THE CASTLE TO THE OLD TOWN

Going south, cross Princes Street to a picturesque uphill path, which takes you for around a kilometre through the eastern part of Princes Street Gardens ➤ p. 42 *to* ❻ Edinburgh Castle ➤ p. 30. Plan approximately an hour for this visit. Then *head down the* Royal Mile ➤ p. 28 *towards the* Old Town ➤ p. 28 *at the bottom.* Is your stomach starting to rumble? ❼ Berties Real Fish & Chips *(9 Victoria Street | 0131 322 1000 | berties fishandships.com) serves top-quality fish and chips in spacious stone-walled premises in picturesque Victoria Street, just a few minutes' walk down the Mile.* On a full stomach, it's now time for a spot of shopping in the Old Town: still in Victoria Street, you can fill your hip flask at the ❽ The Whisky Shop ➤ p. 75 to sip later while watching the evening sunset on Calton Hill. *Just*

❻ Edinburgh Castle

❼ Berties Real Fish & Chips

❽ The Whisky Shop

another 100m downhill, you'll come across the Grassmarket ➤ p. 28 and the cult second-hand store ❾ **Armstrong & Son** ➤ p. 71. *Just a few steps further along is the famous hat shop* ❿ **Fabhatrix** ➤ p. 72.

TARTAN KITSCH AND IMPORTANT SCOTTISH SITES
Back on Victoria Street, return to the ⓫ **Royal Mile** ➤ p. 28. *It may seem like an endless celebration of Scottish myths and tartan kitsch, but there are also many highlights worth visiting such as* ⓬ **St Giles' Cathedral** ➤ p. 32 – *look for the angel playing the bagpipes! – and* ⓭ **John Knox House** ➤ p. 34. *Then continue down the Mile and take your photo with the statue of poet Robert Fergusson (p. 30 and p. 119) and explore the hidden garden in Dunbar's Close right next door. You'll find the modern* ⓮ **Scottish Parliament** ➤ p. 34 *on the eastern end of the Mile, next to the majestic* ⓯ **Palace of Holyroodhouse** ➤ p. 35.

SUNSET HIGH ABOVE THE CITY
Before the sun sets, *go along Calton Road and past the cemetery to climb the grassy volcanic plug* ⓰ **Calton Hill** ➤ p. 44. *At the top of the hill, you'll discover many strange monuments, including the columns of the*

Where the King stays when he visits Edinburgh: Palace of Holyroodhouse

102

DISCOVERY TOURS

unfinished ⓱ National Monument ➤ p. 45. At the right time of year and weather permitting, you can enjoy the fabulous view of the city's skyline and castle at sunset – and sip whisky from your hip flask as you do so. *Slàinte!*

⓱ National Monument

AN EVENING OF FOLK MUSIC
After enjoying the sunset, you're just 1km away from your evening entertainment. *Leave Calton Hill in the direction of the Balmoral Hotel clocktower. Take the Waverley Steps and cross the train station to Market Street. Cross this street and take the spiral staircase called Scotsman Steps.* Artist Martin Creed had the 104 steps built from different types of marble here. *Once you reach the top, you'll be at North Bridge. Walk south via South Bridge to reach Infirmary Street.* Go to ⓲ Mother India's Café ➤ p. 63 for dinner and then enjoy live music at the ⓳ Royal Oak ➤ p. 85 folk bar.

INSIDER TIP: Steps as art

⓲ Mother India Café

⓳ Royal Oak

❷ IDYLL ALONG THE WATER OF LEITH

➤ Enjoy nature close to the city centre
➤ Explore two temples of modern art
➤ Marvel at the *Man on the River*

📍 Raeburn Place
🏁 St Cuthbert's Churchyard
➡ 6km
🚶 4–5 hrs (2 hrs total walking time)
ℹ wateroflleith.org.uk

SURROUNDED BY GREENERY
Your tour begins at ❶ Raeburn Place ➤ p. 70, a street with many small shops. An old barber's, a fishmonger's and second-hand shops invite you to window shop and rummage around. You can also find sandwiches for a picnic at Greggs *(no. 27a)*. With your bag full of

❶ Raeburn Place

103

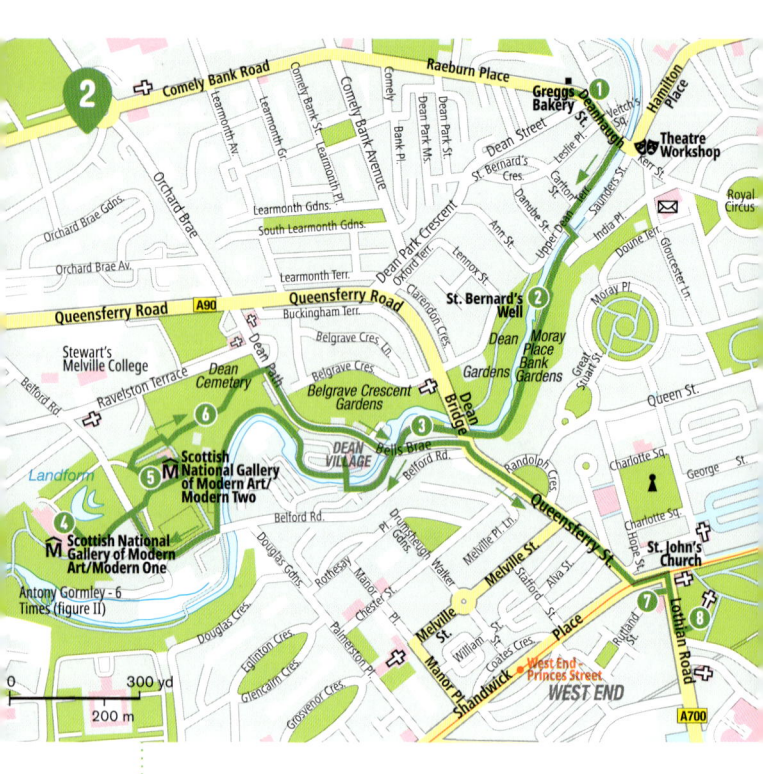

goodies, *stroll down to Kerr Street Bridge, where you then make your way down to the banks of the Water of Leith.* Once there, you'll be surrounded by green. Wrought-iron fencing frames the river banks, which are often frequented by blue kingfishers. You can catch a fleeting glimpse of the old villas up on **Upper Dean Terrace** through the treetops.

A PICNIC BY THE OLD WELL

Stroll along the east bank following the signposts to the galleries and, a few minutes later, you'll be standing in front of ❷ **St Bernard's Well**. The small temple with the figure of Hygeia, the Greek goddess of cleanliness, marks the place where an ancient spring once stood and is the perfect spot to enjoy your pastries. *A little further on, the slender supports of* ❸ **Dean Bridge** *soar into the sky. The riverside route takes you along Miller*

❷ St Bernard's Well

❸ Dean Bridge

DISCOVERY TOURS

Row, along rural lanes with half-timbered houses. Mills and bread ovens were standing here many hundreds of years ago. On some house walls, you'll see a depiction of the paddles used to remove bread from the ovens, which was the emblem of the bakers' guild. *If you now saunter along to the Dean Path/Hawthornbank Lane river crossing*, you'll be treated to a panoramic view of the stone walls of Dean Village ➤ p. 47 – a perfect opportunity for a photo.

INSIDER TIP Classic photo opportunity

MODERN ART FOR AN EXCITING CONTRAST

Cross the small bridge on Dean Path and climb up out of the valley after the river bend to reach the two galleries, designed like classic temples, on Belford Road. If you continue your stroll for another ten minutes along the Water of Leith walkway before going to the galleries, you'll come across the *Man on the River* – a portrait by Antony Gormley and one of a series of standing figures known as *6 TIMES*. The ❹ Scottish National Gallery of Modern Art One ➤ p. 47 and ❺ Scottish National Gallery of Modern Art Two ➤ p. 47 exhibit the most exciting modern and contemporary art and you should consider taking a short break here and enjoying a cup of tea and a piece of cake in one of the cafés. On no account should you miss the sculptures by

INSIDER TIP Gormley sculpture

❹ Scottish National Gallery of Modern Art One

❺ Scottish National Gallery of Modern Art Two

The art is not always hidden behind walls at the Scottish National Gallery of Modern Art

105

Moore and Gormley or the landscape art by Charles Jencks.

ALL ROADS LEAD TO THE CASTLE

Your journey back starts behind Modern Art Two. *Cross the beautiful* ❻ *Dean Cemetery and when you leave, turn right along Dean Path. Once you have crossed the water, you'll reach Dean Bridge again down Bell's Brae. Head southeast along the main road to Queensferry Street.* Halfway down Queensferry Street you'll be confronted with an outstanding example of Edinburgh's various architectural styles in one place: *Melville Street down on the right has a classical feel, with its row of Georgian townhouse façades, while a stylised Gothic church looms up in contrast behind them. After about 200m, you'll reach the splendid bar* ❼ The Huxley *(1 Rutland Street | thehuxley.co.uk) in the Rutland Hotel;* it's well worth popping in for a drink. You're treated to the best view of Edinburgh Castle from the nearby ❽ **St Cuthbert's Churchyard ➤ p. 43**

❸ A LITERARY TRAIL

➤ Make surprising discoveries around the Royal Mile
➤ Take a breather with a literary feel in cafés and pubs
➤ Soak up Old Town atmosphere with a whole lot of history

📍 James Court

🏁 Surgeons' Hall Museums

→ 3km

🚶 2-3 hrs (40 mins total walking time)

ℹ What to pack: reading material from Burns, Stevenson, Rowling and others – if you want to do some reading along the way. Info at *edinburghliterarypubtour.co.uk* and *edinburghbookloverstour.com*

DISCOVERY TOURS

A CELLAR PUB

The walk begins at ❶ James Court. The courtyard is surrounded by pretty residential buildings – this is where the journalist and author James Boswell (1740-95) rented a flat. He had to leave his family behind when he went to look for a publisher for his work in the city. To his dismay, he was forced to work in the legal profession and "rewarded" himself with a free and easy nightlife. The cellar pub ❷ Jolly Judge *(7 James Court)* would have suited him well. Meeting Voltaire and Rousseau were highlights of his life, as was his encounter with England's most celebrated intellectual, Samuel Johnson. The famous diarist and literary critic – and author of the first English dictionary – subsequently set out on an arduous trip to the Outer Hebrides with Boswell in August 1773, which was to last several months. The books written by the two men still make great reading today and are regarded as early travel literature. Take your first pub break here.

INSIDER TIP: Early travel writing

Step back in time: sundown in James Court

❶ James Court
❷ Jolly Judge
❸ Gladstone's Land

17TH-CENTURY HOME DECOR

Head back to the Royal Mile, take a left and enter a three-storey residential building dating from the 17th century, ❸ Gladstone's Land *(daily April-June, Sept, Oct 10am-5pm, July, Aug 10am-6pm, Nov-March guided tours only | admission £10)*. Owned by the National Trust, it gives an insight into how wealthy merchant Gladstone and his tenants once lived. *Return to the Mile and walk to the next street on your left-hand side:* Lady Stair's Close. This is where the Scottish national poet Robert Burns (1759-96) spent a winter.

107

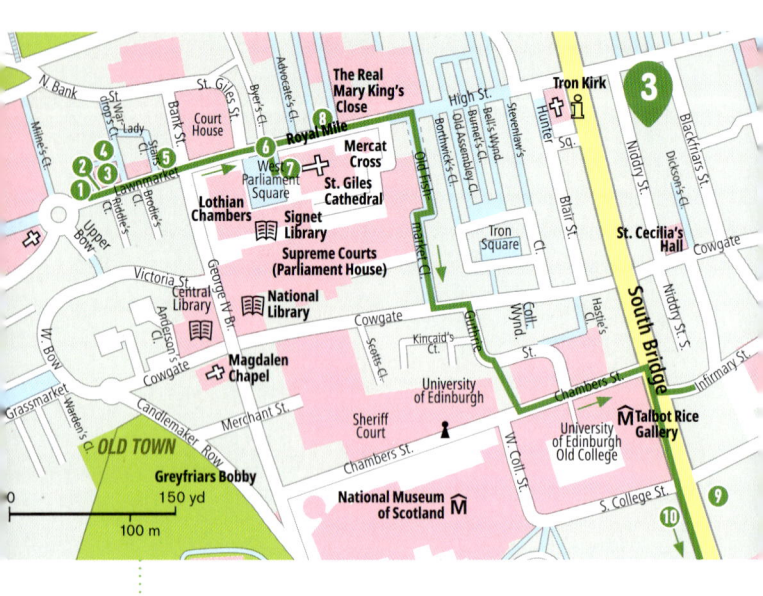

POETRY TO KEEP YOU COMPANY

Burns had just written his first collection of poetry in Scots, influenced by the young, extremely talented Robert Fergusson (1750–74), whose striding bronze statue (p.30 and p. 119) has been erected around a kilometre further along, in the lower section of the Royal Mile ➤ p. 30.

❹ **The Writers' Museum**

❹ The Writers' Museum ➤ p. 32 in Lady Stair's Close is devoted to Edinburgh's most influential writers. At this small museum you can buy a volume of Burns' verse in Scots dialect, which is not too hard to understand.

THE THIEVING JOINER

Back on the Mile, turn left. At the first junction, you have another opportunity for a pub break. This pub,

❺ **Deacon Brodie's Tavern**

❺ Deacon Brodie's Tavern, is named after a joiner and city councillor who stole from his customers at night using duplicate keys. Brodie had his joiner's workshop at Brodie's Close, which is the street diagonally across from the Mile. In 1788, Brodie was hanged from gallows that he had built himself. A hundred years later, Brodie's story inspired Robert Louis Stevenson to write *The Strange Case of Dr Jekyll and Mr Hyde*. The same junction is dominated by the sitting statue of the philosopher David Hume (1711–76). Hume was a political economist, philosopher and historian, and an acquaintance of the market-economy philosopher Adam Smith, a scholar of the Scottish Enlightenment.

WORSHIPPING AUTHORS IN THE CATHEDRAL
Back on the Royal Mile, you're now at the section called Lawnmarket. A few steps down the Mile is the spot where Brodie was hanged at Tollbooth Prison. Now, the site is only marked by the ❻ Heart of Midlothian in the pavement. Here you'll also stumble across the name of Walter Scott, who was the real inventor of Scotland as a tourist destination. His novel *The Heart of Midlothian* (1818) mentions the gruesome prison. *Now turn right to* ❼ St Giles' Cathedral ➤ p. 32 to see how Edinburgh honours its writers: Burns has been given a memorial window and Robert Louis Stevenson is remembered with a sculptured plaque.

❻ Heart of Midlothian

❼ St Giles' Cathedral

HUNGER AND DIRT IN TIMES GONE BY
You should not miss two other lanes opposite the church. On the left, the name of Advocate's Close reminds us

Discuss Dr Jekyll & Mr Hyde over a pint: Deacon Brodie's Tavern

⑥ The Real Mary King's Close

that Stevenson, Scott and Boswell were all lawyers. And a visit to **⑥ The Real Mary King's Close ➤ p. 33** gives an impression of how things were in the year of the plague in 1645, when the street and its people were walled in. A tour shows how the inhabitants of the Old Town fought against hunger, filth and disease. *Now head 50m down the Mile and enter Old Fishmarket Close on your right. Then cross Cowgate, the road that runs parallel to the Mile to the south, and turn into* Guthrie Street *opposite*, where Walter Scott was born.

WHERE LONG JOHN SILVER WAS BORN

At the south end of Guthrie Street, turn left and go over South Bridge to Infirmary Street, where Scott attended the Royal High School, today a university building. This was the site of the Old Royal Infirmary, where the writer William Ernest Henley convalesced for almost two years after undergoing a foot amputation due to tuberculosis. He became the model for the pirate with the wooden leg, Long John Silver, in Stevenson's *Treasure Island*. Stevenson visited his friend regularly in his sick bed. They wrote the drama *Deacon Brodie* together in 1880, which was the precursor of Stevenson's *The Strange Case of Dr Jekyll and Mr Hyde*.

The Elephant House: a meeting place for Harry Potter fans (and everyone else!)

DISCOVERY TOURS

FINISH WITH SURGICAL PRECISION
Back on South Bridge, turn left and you'll soon see the Festival Theatre in front of you – the main home of the Edinburgh International Festival. Opposite, you can drift into ❾ Bagpipes Galore ➤ p. 74 *and browse the woodwind instruments. A few steps later, the* ❿ Surgeons' Hall Museums ➤ p. 38 *will beckon you inside. The famous museum is part of the Royal College of Surgeons. Inside, you'll find striking exhibits and by the end, you'll know all about how surgical research is linked to forensic science and literature. There's a café too.*

❾ Bagpipes Galore

❿ Surgeons' Hall Museums

❹ OVER THE VOLCANO

➤ Strike out on a city walk with a Highlands feel
➤ Marvel at the fantastic views right out to the Firth of Forth
➤ Take a break to visit the oldest pub in Scotland

📍	The Scottish Parliament	🏁	Dr Neil's Garden
→	5.6km	🚶	4–5 hrs (2 hrs total walking time)
📊	easy	↗	approx. 300m

STEP BY STEP FOR THAT HIGHLAND FEELING
Around 200m from the ❶ Scottish Parliament ➤ p. 34, *heading towards Arthur's Seat, you'll reach Queen's Drive. Turn left, and right after about 100m onto a mountain path called Radical Road. The path runs below* ❷ Salisbury Crags, *a procession of imposing 46m-high basalt columns that can be seen from far away. You'll be rewarded with splendid views over the city that get better with each step. Before you return to Queen's Drive, turn sharp left, and then take a left fork again after around 50m to now follow, in the opposite direction to before, a path called Volunteer's Walk heading towards the north. You're now walking along a*

❶ The Scottish Parliament

❷ Salisbury Crags

terrace above the crags. By now you'll have left the city far behind and a Highland hiking feeling will have taken over.

SUBLIME VIEW FROM THE SUMMIT

Leave the swampy area of Hunter's Bog to your right: the view sweeps over the city to the Firth of Forth. *After another 300m, turn right, to the right of the path that curves left, just before reaching Queen's Drive once again.* Your destination is the remains of ❸ St Anthony's Chapel *(undiscoveredscotland.co.uk/edinburgh/stanthonys)*, towering 200m to the east, dramatically exposed above St Margaret's Loch. *Follow the lightly worn paths to this site.* Take a break to enjoy the magnificent panoramic view. Walk southwards again, straight towards the volcanic peak of ❹ Arthur's Seat ➤ p. 37 (251m). *You'll reach the summit around 1km*

❸ St Anthony's Chapel

❹ Arthur's Seat

DISCOVERY TOURS

beyond the ruins. Now you're standing 170m above the start of the route. The view of the Firth of Forth in the distance is amazing.

REFRESHMENTS IN SCOTLAND'S OLDEST PUB
For the descent, take one of the paths towards Dunsapie Loch 500m to the east, then follow one of the trails down to the car park on Queen's Drive at the south end of the loch. The water of ❺ **Duddingston Loch** sparkles a good 200m further south. *Turn right along Queen's Drive in the direction of Duddingston Loch. If you turn off Queen's Drive to the left after 50m, you'll reach The Causeway,* where refreshments beckon at the ❻ **Sheep Heid Inn** ➤ p. 83. It's said that even Mary, Queen of Scots once stopped for a restorative beverage here, in the oldest pub in Scotland. ==A few steps further is an inspiring botanical garden with free admission:== ❼ **Dr Neil's Garden** *(daily 10am–5pm | drneilsgarden.co.uk).* Enjoy the view over the loch as the sun goes down. *Bus 12 (to Holyrood High School) departs from the car park next to the garden and will take you back to the city.*

INSIDER TIP
Secret garden idyll

❺ Duddingston Loch

❻ Sheep Heid Inn

❼ Dr Neil's Garden

A paradise for birds beneah the ruins: St Margaret's Loch by St Anthony's Chapel

GOOD TO KNOW
HOLIDAY BASICS

ARRIVAL

GETTING THERE

Edinburgh is easily accessible by train from the rest of mainland Britain. Direct services leave London King's Cross station roughly every half hour; journey time is around 4 hours 30 minutes. There are also direct services from other cities, including Glasgow and Manchester. Advance fares from London, with trains operated by *LNER* (lner.co.uk) and *ScotRail* (scotrail.co.uk), can be as little as £35 for a one-way ticket, but you need to book well ahead to get low prices. Also see nationalrail.co.uk for times and fares.

Companies including *National Express* (nationalexpress.com), *Flixbus* (global.flixbus.com) and *Megabus* (megabus.com) run regular direct coach services from London to Edinburgh. Journey time is around 8 to 10 hours 30 minutes, and prices start at around £15 for a single ticket.

Time zones

The UK is on Greenwich Mean Time (GMT) in winter, and British Summer Time (BST), which is one hour ahead of GMT, in the warmer months. In summer, Edinburgh is five hours ahead of the North American east coast.

Adaptor Type G

Visitors from abroad will need a plug adaptor. You can buy one for three-pin plug sockets in your home country or in Edinburgh.

Make your way along Princes Street by bus or tram

You'll need to book early to get the cheapest fares.

There are direct domestic flights from London to Edinburgh on budget airlines *easyJet (easyjet.com)* and *Ryanair (ryanair.com)*. Prices can be as low as £20 for a single fare if you book ahead. *British Airways (britishairways.com)* has numerous daily flights. *Ryanair*, *easyJet*, *Aer Lingus (aerlingus.com)* and *British Airways* also offer flights from Belfast to Edinburgh (journey time 55 minutes). Various companies offer ferry services between Northern Ireland and Scotland. See directferries.co.uk for details.

From Ireland, *Aer Lingus* and *Ryanair* have direct flights from Dublin to Edinburgh (journey time around 1 hour 15 minutes). There are direct flights from US cities including Boston, New York, Atlanta, Washington DC and Chicago to Edinburgh, and from Canada direct flights operate from Toronto and Calgary. Flight time from the east coast is around 7 hours.

From the airport, a *tram* to the city leaves every 7 minutes (travel time 30 minutes, fare £7.50). *Airlink 100* operates buses around the clock, with services every 10 minutes during the day and every 15 minutes at night; the fare is £5.50. Night bus N22 travels to the city and Leith between 12.15am and 4am for £3. A taxi costs around £25.

CLIMATE & WHEN TO GO

Edinburgh usually enjoys pleasant weather in summer, with temperatures between 15°C and 25°C. The spring and autumn months are fresher at between 5°C and 10°C. Winters are cool and wet, but it's rare for temperatures to go below freezing during the day. A trip to Portobello Beach is great from June to October if you just want to go for a walk. With water temperatures between 12°C and 16°C, swimming is more enjoyable for people who like cold-water swimming.

The nicest time to visit is from June to September, the months with the most daylight. Winter is much quieter, but more people are beginning to travel at this time of year. The winter sun is very low, lighting things up from an interesting angle.

GETTING AROUND

BICYCLE
Even though a lot of Edinburgh is steep and the roads are not smooth, it's very bicycle-friendly. The network of flat cycle paths is well signposted, surrounded by green, and doesn't have road crossings. You'll find many routes on the website *short.travel/edi29*, as well as additional links highlighting guided and commented tours.

CAR
You can hire a car at the airport. However, everything is so close together in the Old Town and New Town that you really don't need a car. In fact, it can make things more difficult, as parking spaces are hard to come by and uniformed parking wardens will issue a fine to anyone breaking the rules.

PUBLIC TRANSPORT
There's an excellent network of buses *(lothianbuses.com)*. A single ticket costs £2 (£1 for a child), and a day ticket is £5 (£2.50 for a child). Both can be bought with a contactless card or with cash on the bus (if paying with cash you must have the exact money).

You can use the tram *(edinburghtrams.com)* for the same price. There are also options for multi-day and family tickets, including an adult 3-day city zone ticket for £10 (children £9) and a family 3-day city zone ticket for £22, valid for up to 2 adults and 3 children. Buy tickets before you board at tram stops using coins or a debit card. The tram is a great way to travel from the airport, and to Leith and Newhaven. A ticket inspector travels on the tram and will provide you with a ticket for your bike (free of charge): get on in the middle of the tram. The app *Transport for Edinburgh (download at tfeapp.com)* is great.

EMERGENCIES

EMBASSIES & CONSULTATES
CONSULATE OF THE UNITED STATES OF AMERICA
3 Regent Terrace, Edinburgh, EH7 5BW | tel. (44) 131 556 8315 | uk.usembassy.gov/embassy-consulates/edinburgh

CANADIAN HONORARY CONSULATE
Tel. (44) 770 235 9916 | international.gc.ca/country-pays/united_kingdom-royaume_uni

GOOD TO KNOW

CONSULATE GENERAL OF IRELAND
16 Randolph Crescent | Edinburgh EH3 7TT | tel: (44) 131 226 7711 | dfa.ie/irish-consulate/edinburgh

EMERGENCY SERVICES
Police, fire brigade, ambulance: tel. 999
Non-emergency police: tel. 101

ESSENTIALS

ACCOMMODATION
Scotland offers a wide range of accommodation, from castle hotels to country homes, and Edinburgh is no exception. If you want to rent a castle apartment or a historic house in the countryside around Edinburgh, contact the *National Trust (tel. 0131 458 0305 | nts.org.uk)*. You can find a selection of B&Bs at *scotlandsbestbandbs.co.uk* and hotels at *visitscotland.com*.

CITY TOURS
Edinburgh Bus Tours (adults £16, children up to 15 free | edinburghbustour.com) offers three 75-minute tours. *Sandemans New Europe (meeting point: Frankie & Benny's, 130 High Street) | neweuropetours.eu)* provides free two-hour guided tours – you pay what you think the tour was worth. Another company also offers several free two-hour tours per day starting at *154 High Street (10am, 11am, 1pm | edinburghfreetour.com)*.

Customised city walks are available from Beryl and Sean, including day tours into the surrounding area *(triporganiser.net)*. You can find humorous and dramatic literary walks with pub stops at *edinburghliterarypubtour.co.uk*.

CUSTOMS
The allowance when entering the UK from abroad, including from Canada and the US, is 4 litres of spirits, plus 42 litres of beer and 18 litres of wine, and 200 cigarettes. For more information see *hmrc.gov.uk/customs*

DISCOUNTS
Public museums are free, but donations are welcome. Various city passes are available online and are worth exploring. The *Royal Edinburgh Ticket (£65 | 48 hrs)* is great for gaining quick entry to royal sites. There are also the *Edinburgh City Pass (£75 | 2 days)* and the *Scotland Explorer Pass (£44 | 7 days)*. For information, see *edinburgh.org/things-to-do/city-passes*

EVENT INFORMATION
Scotland's daily newspaper *The Scotsman (scotsman.com)* provides information on the times and prices of various events. *The List*'s website *(list.co.uk)* is also a great place to find information.

HEALTH
Post-Brexit, short-term visitors from the EU can still access necessary NHS medical care through the European Health Insurance Card (EHIC). In some cases, you will have to pay directly and submit your bill for refund when you return home. Visitors from other

countries should take out comprehensive medical insurance.

HOW MUCH DOES IT COST?	
Malt whisky	from £39 for a good bottle
Taxi	£17 for 10km
Fish & chips	£6.50–£9.50 for a takeaway
Coffee	£3 for a cup
Tram	£2 for a single ticket
Soup	£6 for a bowl in a pub

INFORMATION
VisitScotland (visitscotland.com) is Scotland's tourism organisation. The tourist information centres are called iCentres. *Edinburgh iCentre (249 High Street | tel. 0131 473 3868).*

LUGGAGE STORAGE
You can book storage for your luggage online here: *short.travel/edi30*. The website lists dozens of places near the sites or key transport hubs. Cost per day is £5.90.

MONEY & CREDIT CARDS
It's easy to withdraw money from cash dispensers at the airport and all over the city using your debit card. Hotels, restaurants and most pubs accept standard debit and credit cards. If you're using a card in a different currency, watch out for bank charges and expensive currency conversion.

Banknotes look different in Scotland than in the rest of Great Britain but have the same value. They are also legal tender in England, though you may run into problems trying to use them. There are £1 notes in circulation in Scotland only, but they stopped being produced in 2001. They're a great souvenir, so don't spend it if you get one!

NATIONAL HOLIDAYS
If Christmas or New Year's Day fall on a Saturday or Sunday, the Monday is a public holiday (known as a "bank holiday" in the UK).

1 Jan	New Year's Day
2 Jan	Bank holiday (banks & institutions closed)
March/April	Good Friday
1st & last Monday in May	Bank holiday
1st Mon in Aug	Bank holiday
30 Nov	St Andrew's Day
25 Dec	Christmas Day
26 Dec	Boxing Day

NEWSPAPERS
Scots love their own newspapers. In Edinburgh, they read *The Scotsman* and in Glasgow they enjoy *The Glasgow Herald*. Of course, you can also get hold of English newspapers.

OPENING TIMES
Most shops are open from Monday to Saturday between 9am and 6pm or 7pm. Sometimes they open for longer on Thursdays. Many shops also open on Sundays (10am–4pm/5pm). Pubs are usually open until at least 11pm every day. Some cafés open as early as 8am.

GOOD TO KNOW

TELEPHONE
The area code for Edinburgh is 0131. For calls from abroad, dial 0044 (the UK code) and then 131. Mobile numbers begin with 077, 078 or 079. Numbers beginning 0800 and 0808 are toll-free; premium rate numbers start with 09. If you're travelling from outside the UK, check roaming charges with your mobile phone provider.

TIPPING
If a service charge is shown on restaurant bills, tips are not expected. If service is not included and you were happy with it, it's usual to leave a 10–12% tip. Hotel staff are always happy to receive a small tip.

WIFI & INTERNET
The vast majority of hotels and many B&Bs provide free WiFi, as do many cafés and bars.

Poet Robert Fergusson strides out on Canongate

WEATHER IN EDINBURGH

■ High season
■ Low season

	JAN	FEB	MARCH	APRIL	MAY	JUNE	JULY	AUG	SEPT	OCT	NOV	DEC
Daytime temperatures	6°	6°	8°	11°	14°	17°	18°	18°	16°	12°	9°	7°
Night-time temperatures	1°	1°	2°	4°	6°	9°	11°	11°	9°	7°	4°	2°
Hours of sunshine per day	2	3	3	5	6	6	5	4	4	3	2	2
Rainy days per month	13	11	11	11	11	12	13	13	12	13	12	13

A sightseeing bus with mighty Edinburgh Castle towering above

HOLIDAY VIBES

FOR RELAXATION & CHILLING

FOR BOOKWORMS & FILM BUFFS

📖 DOORS OPEN
A thriller by Ian Rankin (2008), without his famed Inspector Rebus, about an ingenious theft of a painting.

📖 🎥 TRAINSPOTTING
Novel (1993) by Irvine Welsh that digs deep into the life of drug addicts in Leith; Welsh cut Edinburgh's soul open with his social scalpel. Director Danny Boyle made a hit film adaptation with Ewan McGregor and Robert Carlyle in 1996, followed by *T2 Trainspotting* in 2017.

🎥 GUILT
This fast-paced mystery thriller series (2019–23) satirises Edinburgh. One lie leads to the next, but everyone thinks they're in the right. Lead actor Mark Bonnar's humour, eloquence and charisma are the only things you can rely on.

🎥 THE ANGEL'S SHARE
Director Ken Loach descended into the Scottish petty-criminal milieu in 2012 to film this tale of four young offenders who break into a distillery to steal the most expensive whisky of all time.